BACKSTAGE PASS

THE GRIT AND THE GLAMOUR

JOE MATERA

EMPIRE
PUBLICATIONS

EMPIRE PUBLICATIONS
1 Newton Street, Manchester M1 1HW
© Joe Matera 2021

ISBN: 978-1-909360-92-1

CONTENTS

ACKNOWLEDGEMENTS

This book would not have been possible without the following people, to whom I am eternally grateful. Thank you first and foremost to my wonderful wife Liz for her continued support, love, patience and understanding. Love you.

My thanks also to Ashley Shaw at Empire Publications for believing in my book, and for the encouragement and support given throughout the writing process and to Mick Middles for his friendship over the years, and for the guidance and support given. And a special thank you to Phil Manzanera for writing the foreword and to all the artists I met and interviewed which form the basis of this book. I'm hugely indebted to you all for the generous giving of your time to me over the years and for the privilege to have shared many backstage and on tour adventures with you.

FOREWORD

Being not only a great guitarist but also an accomplished wordsmith, Joe Matera gives us a great insight into the world of Rock and Pop music from the inside, having managed to meet many bands and chat to them casually, as well as touring himself.

I remember our last meeting in Melbourne after our 2011 ROXY gig in Melbourne. He came backstage with a friend and me and my wife Claire approached them with a bottle of Dom Perignon in hand and some glasses. This was my tipple of choice after a gig and now seeing it in writing it seems so Rock 'n' Roll. The truth is that that's the only drink I have during each day of building up to the performance at a show and it helps me come down after the excitement of experiencing what in effect is a communion with an audience of people who want to enjoy the evening as much as we do!

Long may live music continue!

Phil Manzanera
London 2021

PRELUDE: BEGINNINGS

Over the course of my life and career I have been asked many times what was so and so like to interview and hang out with backstage? To most people the perception of the life of a music journalist is one of hanging out at parties with rock stars, partying until the early hours, jetting off to far away locations and indulging in all the glamorous benefits that come with hanging with that sort of crowd. This perception couldn't be further from the truth. Of course, there are writers that do the whole shebang and go to all the parties and whatnot but the majority are like myself, quietly undertaking the arduous task at hand. Writing about music involves long hours spent researching material, transcribing and writing up interviews, putting together articles and meeting a never-ending schedule of deadlines that is part and parcel of this line of work. Yet having said that, it is a total privilege and honour to be blessed with such a career where every day it's just music and meeting your musical heroes.

First and foremost I'm a musician and when it comes to music journalism I never take the path of the kind of journalism that is all about scandal, gossip and grabbing a juicy headline aimed at selling magazines. For me it is always about the music and the artist, everything else is secondary. It's a desire to understand their music – past, present and future.

My earliest memories of music were at the age of four when I saw a copy of The Beach Boys' *Pet Sounds* album in a local record store in my home town of Kyabram, a small rural town in Victoria. Pointing the album out to my mother she bought it for me and I spent many hours listening to it. I also remember having a small transistor radio which I would always have tuned to the local station absorbing the latest hits. At night I would take my radio to bed with me and fall asleep listening to sounds emanating from the airwaves. I was fortunate that my parents had a diverse record collection and, being newly emigrated from Italy, they would purchase the latest imported Italian hits on 45s.

I wrote a lot as a child, mostly just inconsequential things, as I just loved writing. At school English proved to be one of my favourite classes. Being an only child music gave me a haven away from the world outside. My teen years were tough through high school and I couldn't wait to get home to put on my records and lose myself in this magical world. I also devoured all the music magazines, learning about my favourite artists and reading about this glamorous lifestyle. I wanted to know everything about the artist and the music. I would read everything I could find about it, the facts were important to me. I fell into a writing career, it was not something planned - life always throws up surprises and you run with it.

I remember around the age of sixteen I had my guitar in hand and was teaching myself how to play, and this feeling struck me out of the blue. I just knew playing guitar was something that was going to become my life but I had no idea how or where or anything. In fact, I could never have imagined how my life would turn out and I am grateful for having the kind of life and work I have done over the ensuing decades.

★

The aim of this book is to take you behind the scenes on my journey as a journalist and artist on tour. It's a glimpse into a world that is far from the public perception. The blood, sweat and tears of making and performing music is wonderfully told by those who created it and I hope this book can shed a little light on the workings of the business and bring you a little closer to knowing your favourite artists, underneath all the glitter and for want of a better word, celebrity, there lies a normal person like you and I who just managed to get lucky and with talent, perspiration and hard work became another footnote in music's illustrious evolving history.

It all started for me when I began going onto the internet in the early 1990s. Around 1994 I was doing some private guitar tuition at a local school and in the library there the computers were all newly connected to the internet. The medium was in its infancy and not everybody had access to a computer at home as we do today. During my lunch breaks I began looking for music-oriented information and guitar-playing material. In the latter part of the 1990s I finally got my own computer and so got myself connected at home and began reading online music interviews and noticed that a lot of the websites had email contacts. With a burning desire to understand more about the artists and music that I loved, I figured I should contact some artists and ask them questions about their own music.

One such artist was Andrew Gold, of 'Lonely Boy' fame, which was a hit for him in 1977. I remember he kindly offered to answer any questions I had about his music via email. Excited by this I put together some questions and emailed them to him. He answered them all and emailed them back to me a few days later. One of the questions I asked him was the huge influence music from the Sixties and Seventies seemed to have on artists' decades later and wondered why music from that period seemed to be timeless. "I think the Sixties and Seventies was the peak period for the singer songwriter for sure," he replied, "people like Cat Stevens, Randy Newman, Jackson Browne, all good songs, but nowadays it's a slightly different thing, with the recording and arrangement more important than the song, which is why they won't last as oldies. But I'm not bothered by it, as it's a phase and it's new, so I don't want to be like my grandparents saying 'this isn't good like in our day!' I like everything including Rap. I just think it's too narrow these days. I'd like to see Rap and songs, and not just R & B, anything, be successful, but it's the teenager's thing, so viva whatever is going on, you know?"

I had done my first ever interview! It gave me confidence to pursue the field further. Later I came across *Songwriter Magazine* through an online song writing site run by the International Songwriters Association in Ireland and saw that they published interviews so I wrote to them to see if they were interested, although I did not expect any kind of response. I was surprised when they wrote back and not only said they were interested but wanted to publish the interview in their magazine and also pay me! I was over the moon. And that became my very first ever published interview and it inspired me to do further interviews. A fire had been lit.

Soon I began seeking out more interview subjects. They eventually ran a few more interviews of mine and again I got paid – all for doing something I enjoyed immensely. My ambitious streak then kicked in. It was time to approach the big guns, magazines such as *Australian Guitar* and the like. Eventually I secured an interview with

Australian pop-rockers Killing Heidi, who at the time were one of the hottest bands in the country, and I also managed to score an interview with Australian born jazz-fusion guitarist Frank Gambale who was a huge draw for the guitar-playing *cognoscenti*. Both interviews were eventually published in *Australian Guitar* in the early months of 2001.

By then I had moved to Melbourne to focus full time on my writing and music. From there it became my home and my career as a music journalist officially took flight.

1 - HOW YOU REMIND ME

With my big first interview now bringing my name to the attention of record labels and publicists, I was being offered interviews with guitar-based artists from both the rock and metal worlds. These mainly involved a lot of up-and-coming to mid-level acts, and while many of the interviews were a nice balance of phone and face-to-face, it would be my interview with Canadian rockers Nickelback in October 2001 that would secure my reputation with the music *cognoscenti*, in turn allowing me access to some of the biggest names over the next decade.

At the time of their first Australian visit Nickelback were on the verge of breaking through. Around six weeks later they became the biggest band around. Before signing to Roadrunner Records in 1999, a label that predominantly specialised in extreme hard rock and metal, Nickelback had been slogging it out on the circuit with a DIY ethic. The band, comprising Chad Kroeger on lead vocals and lead guitar, his brother Mike on bass, Ryan Peake on rhythm guitar and his cousin Brandon Kroeger on drums, had first started out as a covers band in the early 1990s under the moniker of 'Village Idiot' doing the rounds in the environs of their native Hanna, Alberta. They eventually recorded a demo, *Hesher* (1996), before their independent debut album, *Curb*, financed by a $4000 loan from Chad Kroeger's stepfather, appeared a few months later. In 2002 *Curb* was reissued with new artwork and given an international release by Roadrunner Records. By the time of the band's second album, 1998's *The State,* again self-financed on a budget of $30,000 and with new drummer Ryan Vikedal having replaced Kroeger on drums, the band toured ceaselessly.

"We had fired our managers right in the middle of recording *The State,*" Peake told me. "So, for like a year we promoted and distributed everything on our own, including releasing the album independently. Then finally that summer we'd been solicited by record companies and got picked up by Roadrunner."

One of Roadrunner's A&R's interest was piqued upon hearing a copy of the band's album, he immediately flew out to Vancouver to see the band perform live. Suitably impressed he returned to the label and urged his bosses to sign the band. With the band now signed, marking Roadrunner's first move into the mainstream rock market, the label reissued *The State* in 2000. It was here that the band's fortunes took off. *The State* would garner the band their first taste of commercial success with the album achieving Gold status in both Canada and the United States.

In early 2001 the band entered the studio to begin recording their third album, *Silver Side Up.* Prior to their Australian visit, 'How You Remind Me' had been issued as the album's lead single in July before the album was inauspiciously slated for release on 11th September 2001.

In Australia, as 'How You Remind Me' slowly climbed the charts, Roadrunner made the band a priority and threw all their resources at them. They secured the band three shows; one in Sydney, and two in Melbourne - one at the Mercury Lounge and the other, a live television broadcast at Chapel Off Chapel the following day.

I received an invite from Roadrunner to interview

them and was granted unlimited access to them while they were in town. I had received an advance copy of their album *Silver Side Up* and found the post-grunge sounds very much to my liking. This was a band that definitely warranted the hype. I approached one of my editors at a local magazine and urged him to be the first to run an Australian cover story on the band as I believed they were on the verge of becoming huge. I will never forget the reaction from my editor, "I don't want an unknown band on the cover. Anyway, I don't think they're going to go anywhere". These famous last words would later come to haunt him! That same editor later admitted his regret in having passed on such an historic opportunity.

I caught the band's first Melbourne show at the now defunct Mercury Lounge, located inside the Crown Casino, and spent time with them backstage both before and after the show with my then girlfriend, now wife, Liz. I arrived at the venue with my "Access All Areas" laminate hanging around my neck at around 9pm just as local support band Dreadnought were about to hit the stage. We headed backstage where I found my way to the dressing room where Nickelback were making themselves comfortable and partaking of the drinks rider. After introducing myself we embarked on some small talk to break the ice. Chad, with his bleached corkscrew hair and guitar in hand, strolled confidently up and the down the narrow hallway while doing finger warm ups on his fret board. Label personnel and crew frantically moved to and fro as cigarette smoke permeated the air. As show time drew closer we left the band as they prepared for their performance and took our positions at the side of the stage.

About half an hour later Nickelback made their way to the stage to the deafening applause of a sell-out crowd.

Quickly grabbing their instruments, they launched into their first song and ran through a a set from both their albums *The State* and *Silver Side Up* – it was a solid and extremely loud 70 minute set, after which they left the stage to the roars of "more, more". With the cheers getting louder, the band returned a few minutes later to perform their eagerly awaited encore, 'How You Remind Me', which had now gone Gold in Australia within weeks of release.

Afterwards I struck up conversation with all of Nickelback's crew, especially their guitar tech Kris who shared some wonderful and very "rock 'n' roll" touring stories with me. After the show people had started lining up beside the stage side door hoping to get autographs from the band, and although some managed to achieve this, the affair was cut very short as the band were whisked away by management and record company personnel to their after-show party at the Spy Lounge on an upstairs section of the venue where Liz and I joined them.

The next day we arrived at Chapel Off Chapel, a former church in Prahran that had been converted into a thriving live venue, with its interior providing a more intimate setting for artists and audience. As we entered Nickelback were just finishing their soundcheck, and with all preparations for their performance later that night now ready, I was led by the publicist to one of the band's backstage dressing rooms to interview guitarist Ryan Peake with whom I sat down with for an enjoyable 25-minute chat. Peake was enthused about the band's inaugural Australian jaunt. "It's great to come to Australia and play sold-out shows first time over" he told me. Afterwards, Peake kindly invited Liz and I to join him for a meal. Later that evening we returned to the concert room to take our seats and watch the band record a live set for an upcoming TV broadcast. The Australian tour saw the band take a break from their current US tour, to which they would return when they got back to the US. It had been a rough month for the band in the aftermath of the 9/11 attacks. Chad Kroeger shared his feelings with the audience on having to decide whether or not to perform a show at a state fair in Pennsylvania on the night the attacks occurred. In the end he decided to go ahead with the show believing it would help the audience end one of the country's darkest days on a more positive note. "It helped turn their minds off what was on CNN and alleviated the tension and everyone just rushed to the front of the stage, and we had a great rock show."

This performance saw a shorter set of songs with 'Too Bad', 'Where Do I Hide', 'How You Remind Me', 'Never Again' and a special acoustic version of 'Leader Of Men', receiving an airing with a question and answer segment added as an intermission. And with that, the band's first Australian tour came to an end.

By the time I got to catch up with the group again in October 2002, the band had well and truly become the biggest rock band on the planet. You couldn't turn on a radio station without hearing 'How You Remind Me'. According to Nielsen SoundScan that song had earned the honour of being the most played song on US radio during the 2000s.

This time I was scheduled for an afternoon interview with Mike Kroeger, the band were in town to perform at the M–ONE festival being held at Colonial Stadium. Since their last visit Kroeger's dyed blonde hair colour had returned to its normal dark colour and was cut shorter. Considering how hectic the past twelve months had been with the constant touring and promotional duties, Kroeger looked fit and healthy and seemingly content with how life was turning out for the group. In the aftermath of the band's fast trajectory to international success, they had also started to attract a lot of negative publicity mainly due to the critics' derision of their formulaic and generic brand of rock fuelled by numerous internet memes that saw Nickelback becoming rock's whipping boys.

With the hotel a hive of noisy activity we decided to go into one of the quieter dining areas in order to conduct my interview. The publicist left us to it but returned a few minutes later with a glass of wine for each of us. Mid way through our interview Chad Kroeger walked into the room having ventured down from his hotel room. I welcomed him back to the country; his long flowing blonde locks were still very much evident and we made small talk. I told him of my joy at seeing that the band had finally made the cover of UK's *Kerrang!* after what the magazine had initially written about them. It seemed like they had finally done a backflip and jumped on the Nickelback bandwagon having panned the band relentlessly for months. Chad's reply to my comment was a firm, "I hate fuckin' *Kerrang!*"

Mike Kroeger told me that his band and members from some of the other international acts that were sharing the festival bill, and who were staying at the same hotel, were planning to spend a night out on the town together at the city's casino complex. Kroeger said he loved it there as he had won $900 the previous night adding that the day after the band's festival appearance they were heading straight back home as he had a 17-month old baby but while Peake was also desperately missing home, Chad had decided to stay in town for a short vacation. Once the group returned to Canada they were scheduled to return to the road to finish their world tour which would end a few weeks before Christmas. After the interview was over we all said our goodbyes and headed downstairs to grab a bite and sip a few more wines before leaving the hotel for their night out. As I walked out to head home, a waiter with a curious look in his eye approached me and enquired, 'what band were they?'

Nickelback's performance at the festival the following day showed how much they had changed since their first tour twelve months prior. The constant touring and the success they'd achieved had moulded the group into a highly polished live act. Chad, ever the consummate performer, held the audience in the palm of his hand for the entire set before closing with their anthemic signature song that saw the stadium singing along to every word.

Nickelback's commercial success continued through a succession of albums and in 2005 Vikedal was replaced with Daniel Adair. The group became the goose that lay the golden egg for Roadrunner, generating huge profits for the label and in 2007 the company was bought out by Warner, but even they couldn't hold on to Nickelback who left the company and would later sign a new multi-million dollar deal with Live Nation.

2 - ACE OF SPADES: LEMMY

Rock stars today have got nothing over those of the halcyon years of rock 'n' roll. Back then they were like Gods, larger than life; fans aspired to be like them, they were untouchable, their music divine. Yet the changing of the guard and the constant evolution of the music industry has changed all of that. These days rock stars, if you want to call them that, are mere celebrities, spruiking their wares and brand to an ever-fragmented audience. Their large and fragile egos are betrayed by their tweets – their constant need for attention seem to take priority over the music. Over the years I can recall a number of times when I was in the presence of a 24 carat rock star. On this occasion it was vocalist and bassist Ian 'Lemmy' Kilmister, the hard living, no holds barred, full throttle main man of English speed demons Motörhead and, just like the band's music, Lemmy truly lived fast and wild. He was the epitome of what constitutes a rock star.

It was such a shock when the news filtered through that Lemmy had passed away a few days after Christmas 2015 and a few days after he had just turned seventy. It was a shock to not only me but to millions of his fans around the world but then he lived fast and was always true to himself. The midnight oil he had been burning for most of his life suddenly flicked out that fateful day. Gone was one of our generation's real legends.

I have many fond memories of Lemmy having first met him in 2005 while he was on tour down under. I first interviewed him back in August 2005 on the phone. These interviews are usually conducted as part of a promotional activity, and usually when an artist is about to release a new album or in this case when they've announced a tour and are doing the promotional rounds in order to spruik the upcoming tour and ticket sales. Prior to doing the interview I had been warned by some fellow music writers that Lemmy was notorious for not suffering fools gladly or for having little patience with lazy journalists who didn't know their shit or were only after a headline. So, with this at the back of my mind, I made sure I researched well, came up with interesting questions and covered topics that would engage the speed rock 'n' roll meister. Armed with my questions, I ventured forth into Lemmy's lion's den.

Straight away the interview seemed to be in reverse as he put me through my paces but I passed Lemmy's exam and won him over to the point where we ended up chatting far beyond the allocated 20 minutes. Our conversation was punctuated by bouts of hearty laughter from Lemmy whose innate sense of humour was evident in his responses to my questions. Having broken the ice he was soon regaling me with tales from life on the road with Motorhead such as this one – "We were going across Croatia in the middle of the night in this fuckin' blizzard, when suddenly Phil [Campbell, Motörhead guitarist] shouts out 'right that's it, I'm leaving. You guys are all cunts. Stop this van now as I've got my suitcase packed'. So the driver pulls over and Phil opens the door, walks out and steps right into three feet of snow! And this blizzard is coming down heavy and there are no lights or anything. The only light we could see was about 40 miles away across the valley. But then all of a sudden that light suddenly went out! You couldn't have timed it better as Phil got back in the van and stayed on!"

Lemmy was never one to mince his words. At the time

of my interview rumours were rife on the internet that he was bisexual, something that was later proven to be completely false. "That was a story put out by a fellow who will not do it again 'cause I had a little chat with him, you know" Lemmy stated matter-of-factly. "The thing is, putting something out like that about somebody else could ruin their fuckin' life. These people are so fuckin' irresponsible. They don't give a fuck about the people they write about. They don't care if they send them to the big house or the gallows. They don't care as long as they get their headline. Believe me this guy won't be doing that again. And if he does it again, I'll be putting a screwdriver through his knee cap!" His response spoke volumes of the type of person he was; Lemmy cared for others, for his fans, for his friends. He had a heart of gold but if you crossed him then watch out!

Lemmy was truly one of the greats, a man described by a friend of mine as "a complete one off". He was the real deal and a true gentleman and demanded the ultimate respect but then this was a fellow who oozed the wild spirit of rock 'n' roll as a natural heir to the hellraising Bluesmen of the 50s and 60s. In his 50 plus years of playing music he never once succumbed to the whimsical greed of the record industry's demands. While musical fads came and went, Lemmy and his motley fellow brothers in Motörhead forged ahead, never diverting from who they were and their *modus operandi*. The speed demon was unstoppable, like a bullet from a sniper's gun. When I asked him about the secrets to his longevity he would joke, "I've got a body that's preserved in alcohol. It's as simple as that".

As our interview came to a close Lemmy remarked: "that was a good one (interview). You asked really good questions Joe, you're a good interviewer". Not only did I feel a sense of pride, having a comment like that come from a person of Lemmy's standing who must have been interviewed a million times, but it was the ultimate endorsement. What surprised me further was when Lemmy requested I meet up with him when Motörhead came to town in December for their latest Australian tour, which would see them paired alongside that other rock 'n' roll circus, Mötley Crüe.

It was a very warm Monday evening when I arrived at the Motörhead-Mötley Crüe show at the Vodafone Arena [since renamed Melbourne Park] in Melbourne. Motörhead had just hit the stage first as part of the double bill and as the first song powered off, the Motörhead beast was smokin' big time. In fact, their set that night blew the Crüe right off the planet. So far their Australian shows had all seen this sort of reaction from fans. It had been fourteen long years since the 'Head last toured down under, and for many it was fourteen years too long. Since Lemmy had invited me backstage, his camp issued me tickets to the show as well as an after show pass. I enjoyed the mighty 'Head's 50 minute set. It's probably the loudest concert I've ever been to and even with ear plugs inserted, my ear drums were still feeling the onslaught days later. At one point Lemmy took to the microphone and addressed his audience, "Is it loud enough for ya?" as soon as the audience heard this they went into a frenzy.

Lemmy's people had instructed me and a handful of others who had also been invited to meet the other members of the band, to wait at the box office once Motörhead's show was over. The set included (though not in any exact order); *Dr. Rock, Stay Clean, Killers, Metropolis, Over The Top, No Class, In The Name Of Tragedy, I Got Mine, Sacrifice* (which included an awesome drum solo from

Mikkey Dee), *Going To Brazil, Killed By Death* – one of my all-time favorite Motörhead tracks – *Ace Of Spades* and finale *Overkill*.

Not long after I was ushered into the backstage area and into the Crüe's large, but at that precise moment quiet, catering room. I waited while Lemmy chilled out for a while in his dressing room after the show. I took a good look around the dressing rooms backstage, and noticed that Mötley Crüe's quite large dressing room had been named "Vincent Von Cock".

From backstage I could hear screams as Mötley Crüe hit the stage and proceeded to unleash their hits-laden set. The sound from the band rippled through the walls of the venue seeping through to the backstage area. In the meantime Motörhead drummer Mikkey Dee popped by to say hello to a couple of people waiting in the room. He had a towel wrapped around his shoulders as he slowly dried the sweat off his brow and his hair. I introduced myself and a bit of small talk followed by a quick photo before Dee departed with a few others to the quiet seclusion of his dressing room.

Then the moment had arrived. I was summoned into Lemmy's dressing room and there was the legend himself drinking (what else!) Jack Daniels whilst being kept company by a stripper, who remained quietly in the corner during the whole time I was there. "Would you like a drink? There's beer or Jack Daniels" he asked, making me feel comfortable and very welcomes. For the next hour I was graced by his presence, wit and kindness. The man was not only the epitome of what a real rock star was and is, but also a true gentleman to boot and very accommodating. As Lemmy and I conversed The 'Head's guitarist Phil Campbell walked through the hallway and as he passed Lemmy's dressing room and he popped his head in to say hi and Lemmy introduced us. Meanwhile, I continued to sink the Jack Daniels, savouring every bit of the moment with the ultimate rock star himself. The man looked healthy and very fit. He was due to turn 60 in a couple of weeks yet looked nowhere near that age. Obviously the rock 'n' roll lifestyle had been good to him, though I did notice a subtle shake in his hands.

Lemmy was full of wit, he was a very well read man, and an avid reader of history, "*A History of Britain*" he told me was one of his favourite reads. I asked him if he listened to any music while he is out on tour? "No" came his reply. Lemmy next displayed his creative flair and his ingenious approach to individuality. He stood up and walked to the small table that was sitting in the corner of the room. A new black t-shirt was spread across the table. He picked up a pair of scissors and proceeded to demonstrate to me a custom job on the garment, something he did often he explained, before adding, "You don't want somebody else to be wearing the same thing as you!" Fashion tips from Lemmy! After he had finished, I handed him a copy of *Australian Guitar* that contained the interview I'd done with him a few months back over the phone. He pulled out a seat, sat down and began to read it while continuing to talk to me.

Our conversations took surprising turns. At one point he discussed spirituality, "Just treat others as you would want to be treated yourself". Ah, words of wisdom from the master himself, so simple yet so timeless. On other musicians and artists he had met he said "Steve Vai and Dave Grohl from the Foo Fighters are the nicest guys in music I've ever met and known". With my curiosity now piqued I asked him if he had met any assholes along the way. "Jet

Harris [*The Shadows' bass player*]" he affirmed categorically.
What about Gene Simmons from KISS I asked, who had
garnered a similar kind of reaction from those who had
met him? "Gene has never said anything bad about me
or done anything to me but I can understand why people
would perceive him as a cunt". I then inquired about his
famous white boots, "I bought them in Los Angeles for
around $500" he admitted me, "they were custom made
for me. The ones I'm wearing tonight [he was wearing a
pair of new knee high black boots, with his black denim
jeans tucked into them] are also made for me". All the
while Lemmy had a cigarette in hand, and in between puffs
he took further sips from his bottle of Jack Daniels. As we
neared the end of our time together he was eager to tell
me that I needed to catch the Crüe's encore. It was not to
be missed he assured me before explaining that a kangaroo
was brought onstage during the set.

"A Kangaroo?" I answered sounding quite puzzled and
mystified. The Crüe's set had a carnival atmosphere and
included strippers, midgets, pyrotechnics... the works really,
but a Kangaroo? Surely this couldn't be for real but with
The Crüe's reputation I wouldn't have put anything past
them. And as if by synchronicity, Lemmy suddenly called
out, "See there's one there, I told you", pointing me in
the direction of the hallway that faced his dressing room.
I took a look around and there was a midget dressed in
a kangaroo suit walking past the dressing room. It was so
funny that we both broke out into laughter.

As has been said time flies when you're having fun and
good things must come to an end and an hour had just
flown by so we said goodbye and I thanked Lemmy for
giving his time. As I began to make my way back out back
into the arena to catch the Crüe's finale, Lemmy offered

me another invite. This time it was to come back and join the after party entourage later in the evening at one of the city's popular strip joints.

I declined but it looked like it was going to be a very long night for some…

3 - I'M NOT DEAD YET - P!NK!

It's May 2007, a mild sunny Autumn day in Melbourne and, being a Wednesday, the working week is in full flight. Tonight though the city will be 'invaded' by American pop star P!NK as part of the Australian leg of her phenomenally successful *I'm Not Dead Yet* world tour. P!NK, born Alecia Beth Moore, adopted her stage name from the character "Mr. Pink", the luckless informant in the notoriously violent Quentin Tarantino film *Reservoir Dogs* and this tour set a record for a female artist in Australia, playing to over 307,000 people.

That afternoon as I made my way to Rod Laver Arena, a 16,000 venue that usually hosts the Australian Open tennis, to hook up with Justin Derrico, P!NK's touring guitarist who will be my chaperon today as well as giving me a behind the scenes look at the workings of a world tour which comes across as a huge travelling circus with stops on every continent on the planet.

Upon making my way through the underground parking area and backstage areas, there are several semi-trailers parked in tandem, which clearly shows the amount of equipment and gear needed for this all-encompassing arena tour. Riggers are putting the final touches on the stage structures to make sure everything is firmly in place, while a large sound crew are rushing back and forth setting up the gear. All around a swarm of people are frantically making sure everything is running to schedule in time for sound check which is planned for around 5.00pm. On a tour of this magnitude everything must run like

17

clockwork and to time. If anything falls behind schedule or some technical fault arises, the chain effect will ripple through every part of the show and should the show start late it can cause it to go over curfew, a costly outcome for the promoter. Last minute technical hitches can mean a scramble to source equipment and an army of technicians and engineers have to plan for every contingency. It is quite an operation. Somehow every possible scenario is allowed for and there's a sense that whatever happens, the show must go on!

My first port of call is Derrico's guitar tech Tony who greets me upon entry to the Arena. He ushers me into the venue via the backstage area entrance. P!NK performed here last night, so everything is already setup from the previous night's show. He gives me a tour of the backstage and stage areas so I can get an idea of the huge scope of the show. He then leads me to an underground stage area directly beneath what has been designated the B Stage area (a smaller secondary stage, which is usually located in the middle of the concert floor connected to the main stage by a walkway). This is where a couple of acoustic guitars are housed for the "acoustic" segment in the show. Tony explains the gear and guitar set-up that Derrico uses for the show. I even get to play some of the guitars. Next we move to his work area which is where he restrings the guitars, and any repairs that may need to be done before, during and after the show.

Finally Derrico arrives on the scene. We greet one another and start chatting. He tells me he's only just woken up; late afternoon starts have become the norm for him, aside from the shows and late night after-show parties he has been on the road for the past year with P!NK and there is another six months to go so it is a very tiring and gruelling schedule with another 15 dates in Australia, a date in New Zealand and then three more legs in Europe, Asia and Africa that would eventually see the tour wind up in Cape Town in September.

One by one each of P!NK's backing band start arriving at the stage area to prepare for sound check. As they filter on stage Derrico introduces them, they are very polite and friendly, there is a sense of family with them all. The amount of time on the road means bonds are formed and friendships made, by default they become a family away from home.

Derrico and I strike up a good conversation before it is decided to go to the boys dressing room – a large designated space backstage that features a large room, along with an adjoining changing room with bathroom and toilets - where we sit down for a good chat. He tells me that to keep his boredom levels low on the long tour, he has taken to studying the guitar further and more intensely. A thirst for knowledge and going beyond the simplicities of pop music has seen him seek to master his instrument and explore its unlimited potential, a source of his passion and desire. He opens a bag filled with loads of instrumental guitar study books from improvisation to chordal workouts. All the while he speaks to me he has a guitar in his hand and is quietly playing scalar runs. He pulls out a black book which contains his itinerary for the tour and hands it to me before rolling a cigarette.

Back on stage he runs through his gear set up for me and plays some guitar to demonstrate his sound. He carries a large variety of instruments with him on the road, I can see eight in total - with a cigarette at a just-so angle between his lips, shoulder length curly blonde hair and flared jeans, he looks like the epitome of cool.

Justin is soon asked to join his band mates as sound check is due to commence so he leaves me and gets back on stage. He starts playing a recognizable riff, which segues into a Led Zeppelin number which quickly sees the drummer join in and the whole place erupts into a massive wall of sound. As I listen to the jam which prepares everyone for the sound check, I look around to the side of the stage and observe a crew member playing with a remote control car. He picks up the remote control car and jumps on stage too, which sees everyone fall about laughing as they join the frolics of chasing the car from one end of the stage to the other. It's scenes like these that help keep things light hearted on long tours.

I move to the mixing desk and watch the sound engineer at work. I am given a set of headphones to listen to the sound check mix. The afternoon has slowly started to get away from us all, as the hours tick closer to dinner time and with the band having run through the music, P!NK finally enters the stage area. Her presence oozes energetic appeal. Dressed in tight Lycra pants, that snugly fits her small but well defined youthful physique, and a black hat that adds a touch of designer chic, she informs the crew and band that because she had a good performance last night and is feeling good, she has decided that there will be no need for her to sound check with the band. A few moments later she heads back to her dressing room.

With the band sound check now over and dinner time looming everyone heads back stage. I am invited to make myself at home and have dinner with the crew. The catering for the tour is taken care of by an in-house chef and his staff. There is an array of food that caters for all diets; vegan, vegetarian and carnivore. I sit down and indulge in a selection of gourmet sausages. The dining area is filling up with crew, all taking their seats to sit down for their well-earned dinner. I enjoy the food, drink and conversation with everyone. Much talk and laughter fills the room. War stories are shared about touring experiences. Derrico shares the tale of an incident that happened on the European leg of the tour last year, at a show in Newcastle, England where he got into a fight and injured his shoulder. Ouch! He had just visited the tour's in-house masseur, straight after sound checking to have a shoulder massage to help him get through the show without any pain which has still been troubling him since.

P!NK comes into the catering area and sits next to us and I am introduced to her. "Nice to meet you Joe" she says as we exchange handshakes. She turns and asks Derrico if she could have a puff of his cigarette. He obliges. She stays to chat with us for a while longer. She then suddenly pulls out her leg and shows us her foot, which looks bruised and is as red as a beetroot, informing us she had hurt it on one of the glass doors earlier. "I must not be alive because there is no blood coming out" she tells us jokingly. She leaves to go and get it tended to and to prepare for the show later in the evening. An hour passes quickly.

With dinner over we all head back again to the "Boys Room". Derrico grabs an acoustic lying on the sofa in the room and makes his way to the toilets where he takes a seat and runs through more finger exercises. The ambience of the room provides a magnificent natural ambient tone to his six-string meanderings. We continue chatting the whole time he's playing away, but it's not long before it is time for him to be on his own. I leave the room to allow him time to prepare for the show.

Outside in the venue, the doors swing open and people start filing in, making their way to their seats in the enormous arena. A couple hours later it is filled with a young crowd impatiently waiting for the show to begin. In the meantime they're being warmed up and entertained by a local support band. I take a seat side of the stage and watch proceedings from there.

After the support act has ended there is a short intermission before the house lights are dimmed. Music is piped through the house PA system as P!NK's band take their positions on stage. Once in position P!NK hits the stage and the place erupts into a deafening sound of cheering and applause. Taking a look around the Arena, the audience is quite diverse and there is a cross section of age groups from the very young to the old, with a predominance of females. P!NK is highly energetic, animated and supercharged and during the show performs several costumes changes. She performs acrobatic moves, which sees her flung high in the air at times. She even comes out on a Harley Davidson during one song and in another she has changed into a bikini.

In the middle of the show things quiet down a little for the acoustic segment. P!NK is joined by her two female backing singers and Derrico on acoustic, sits down on the Stage B area and performs a laid back set which includes the show stopper, 'Dear Mr. President'. The finale sees P!NK and her dancers dressed in outfits made of mesh, navigating more acrobatic movements in mid-air before coloured confetti is let loose and flies all over the venue amid the screams of fans for more. She returns for an encore of two songs to cap off the night's performance. Everyone heads backstage to come down and ready themselves for their return to their hotels. The band and crew will be up early the next morning to take a flight for their show in Adelaide. I am invited back in two weeks, when the show returns for their final Melbourne show.

Two weeks later I return to Rod Laver Arena, arriving in late afternoon. I drive into my allocated VIP parking space at the back of the arena. Making my way to the back stage area, I notice the stage is still mid-way through being set up due having been brought down from Sydney, where P!NK performed her show the previous night. As I watch proceedings, I strike up a conversation with the stage manager/rigger who shares some war stories with me such as his experiences working with American superstar Neil Diamond ("a nice guy who gets his crew, band and himself all flown around the US in a single plane") and other acts such as The Counting Crows and Third Eye Blind. He tells me he has only been home a few times for about a week in total during this lengthy P!NK tour which will soon head to Europe. Touring can take a toll, especially when it comes to personal relationships and domestic duties and successful tours like this have a habit of being extended as shows are added to cope with demand.

Sound check is later than usual as things are currently running slightly behind schedule. When sound check begins, the band runs through a few numbers in portions before P!NK turns up. This time she stays and joins the band. So I am treated to a great "intimate" concert as P!NK and her band perform in front of a handful of engineers and one lucky journalist! This is a lot closer than any of her audience will get during her show; even in rehearsal her vocals are supremely strong and authentic. It was a real privilege.

After sound check it's back to the dressing room. I begin a conversation with the band's drummer who tells me he has played with Slash who he describes as "one of the nicest guys around, although he is always smoking, no matter where he is!" I eat my meal with the other band members and crew. Tonight's meal comprises king fish fillet and vegetables. Stories are again shared around the table. One of the crew informs us he was also a stunt guy for the *Matrix 2* movie. After much food, drink and conversation show time is getting closer and I say my goodbyes and allow them the space and private time to prepare.

It's a sell out once again and there doesn't seem to be a spare seat to be had. I take my position at the side of the stage in the guitar zone where guitars and the guitar tech's work bench stands, which gives me a superb view of everything. Standing nearby is Australian singing legend Daryl Braithwaite who has come along as a back stage guest. One of the box-office people passes on information to the admin office informing them that P!NK has just clocked up 300,000 in ticket sales thus far. The tour will eventually gross $41 million.

When P!NK hits the stage the response is deafening and she performs the exact same show as on her last Melbourne visit two weeks earlier. With a curfew in place everything ends at the allotted 11pm finish under a massive loud roar of approval. P!NK has flown her husband in from the United States, so she leaves the backstage area quickly to join him and disappears into the night.

Two years later, in July 2009, I was again invited to spend time with P!NK and her band and crew while they were in town this time as part of their worldwide *Funhouse* tour. Following the phenomenal success of the 06/07 tour, P!NK spent more than three months criss-crossing Australia in 2009 and *Funhouse* grossed more than $80 million. She played 58 shows in Australia and that leg of the tour broke the record for the biggest tour in the history of the country, which is quite a remarkable achievement for any performer.

On the day of the show I again made my way to Rod Laver Arena in the early afternoon and met up again with Justin Derrico. With it being show day the arena was a hive of activity. After a welcoming hug, we headed for the stage. They were now about 70 shows into the *Funhouse* tour that P!NK had begun earlier in the year and which Derrico informed me would end the following summer. He introduced me to his new guitar tech Chet. The Funhouse set was being put together and the crew were frantically working on it and preparing it in time for the band's sound check later that afternoon. I got chatting to Chet and during our conversation he mentioned that he knew me from my writing.

"I have to ask you something, man. Do you remember an interview you did with John 5 (guitarist for Marilyn Manson and Rob Zombie) about four years ago?"

"Yep, I got him to do a special guitar lesson for *Australian Guitar* magazine".

"Well, you know there were these photos…"

"Yeah, I asked John 5 to get me photos of his hands on his guitar for the fingering instructional pics to go with the lesson for the magazine".

"Yeah those hands" he said waving at me.

I suddenly looked at his hands and realising they looked familiar said, "they were your hands!"

"That's right. John 5 asked me to do it for him, so I got my fingernails coloured like his, wore the same sleeves and took the photos."

"Amazing nobody ever noticed. What a funny story."

As we continued chatting he told me he'd been guitar

teching for Slash and that he had also guitar tech-ed for Eddie Van Halen and a number of other bands too.

Derrico and I made our way to his and the band's spacious dressing room backstage at Rod Laver Arena, which was the same place I was in the last time I was there and we sat down and did a 45 minute interview. Derrico enthusiastically brought up a few tracks on his laptop that he had recorded on the current tour that he wanted me to listen to. Among the tracks there was an instrumental that he wrote and dedicated to Alecia, the real name of P!NK and what he called her since she was his boss.

Clothes, shoes and travel bags were strewn around the room. He also showed me a pair of really cool cowboy boots that he had picked up in Hollywood. He also revealed that the band and crew recently had a week off while in Australia where P!NK took all the crew and band to Port Douglas, in the tropical far north of Queensland for a well-deserved break. Derrico also mentioned that his girlfriend was with him on this tour, on the previous Australian tour she had been one of the dancers. This time though she was just tagging along with Derrico and doing her own thing. He told me that the last *Australian Guitar* article I did on him was stuck on his mum's wall back home.

We headed back out on stage where band members were filtering in for sound check. A few even recognized me from last time. One of the crew guys came up, shook my hand and told me he remembered me and then added, "Mark (Mark Schulman, P!NK's touring drummer) said to tell you that you look like Joey Kramer [Aerosmith drummer] who is one of Mark's friends". "That's cool", I replied, and then looked out towards Mark who was onstage before his drum kit, pointed to him and gave him a smile. Derrico got onstage to start sound checking with violinist

Jessy Greene accompanying him. The Musical Director of the band then took charge of sound checking and for a lengthy time they simply went over and over a piece they were working on, trying some different arrangements which they hoped to perform on P!NK's upcoming US tour. They sound checked for a solid ninety minutes or so but P!NK didn't surface, not that she needed to. Apparently, like last time, her husband had just left Australia for the U.S after having being here for a couple of months. Derrico told me he was only allocated eight tickets for the entire Australian tour and kindly kept two passes for my wife and I so we could see the show later that evening.

With dinner time nearing, I left the Arena to have meet my wife and left Derrico to enjoy his dinner, relax and ready himself for show time. The show didn't begin until thirty minutes later than scheduled, and so ended up running late and finishing way past curfew which would incur a fine from the local city authorities. Derrico later confided in me the reason for the lateness; P!NK and band were having a quiet prayer backstage and started chatting with each other before realizing they had a show to do!

When they finally hit the stage it was one hell of a show. One thing I noticed this time around compared to the last shows in 2007, there were loads more guitar solos and about half a dozen covers included in the set. These ranged from The Divinyls' 'I Touch Myself' (where P!NK sat on a couch and multiple hands started coming up through the couch touching her) to Led Zeppelin's 'Babe, I'm Gonna Leave You' (where Derrico performed a lengthy, high-energy guitar solo) to Gnarls Barkley's 'Crazy' and due to the lateness of the show, the encore ran immediately without a break.

4 - DEATH 'N' ROLL

It's just gone midnight and Swedish producer/engineer and Sunlight Studios owner Tomas Skogsberg gets me to do a final vocal take on a track of mine we have been working on for the past six hours. Having already laid down drums and acoustic guitars and now lead vocals, it's been a marathon effort. I'm here on my latest Swedish tour spending two days between shows at the famed birth place of Swedish Death Metal. Located about an hour's drive north east of Stockholm, the unassuming studio sits quietly in the Swedish forest. The converted barn-cum-studio has, for the past three decades, quietly churned out a signature sound that's become the template for what has become known as the 'Sunlight Studio Sound'.

It's a different world here, and with echoes of the past. The studio grounds houses Tomas' residence a few hundred yards away and a small bungalow. Modern luxuries are forgone, there is no television or Wi-Fi while the old school living quarters lend themselves to focus on the work at hand; creating music. We live in a world where everything is taken for granted – we expect the latest gadgets to be on hand at our beck and call - so it is a bit of culture shock to adjust to life without them and realise how attached we are to our technology.

Within hours of getting here I already felt less stressed. The quiet and calm of the surrounding forest soothes my soul, I am a world away from home, yet strangely I feel at home here. My creativity is fuelled, my imagination fired, I feel privileged to be working alongside Tomas. The man is a legend, a quiet achiever, a man who has made an incredible contribution to Swedish music that all began for him back in the 1980s.

In December 1989 a newly formed group of musical misfits out of Stockholm going under the moniker of Entombed entered local recording facility Sunlight Studios to record their debut album, *Left Hand Path*. Helming production and engineering duties was the studio's owner, a young Swedish guy named Tomas Skogsberg who encouraged the band to experiment with a guitar distortion effect pedal appropriately called Heavy Metal. By cranking all the knobs to maximum they discovered a heavily distorted harsh guitar sound – labelled the 'buzzsaw' sound - which to the ear sounded like a swarm of bees, yet at the same time sounded very unique. Skogsberg's left-field recording approach and sonic exploration soon gave birth to what became known as Swedish Death Metal. When the album was released the following year its new sound, featuring pummelling rhythms and growling vocal melodies, was met with acclaim and proved influential, firmly entrenching Skogsberg and Entombed into the annals of music history.

Swedish-born Skogsberg found the music of The Beatles a life changing event at a very young age. Becoming particularly fascinated with the group's studio opus *The White Album,* he soon developed an interest in all things related to studio recording. His burgeoning passion would be further fuelled when he stumbled upon Black Sabbath's *Sabbath Bloody Sabbath* and Deep Purple's *Machine Head* albums. Immersing himself in the albums, his life in metal was sealed. At the same time the contemporary DIY punk-rock sounds of the day would inspire him to experiment with his own makeshift recordings during his teenage years. He eventually started Sunlight Studios in 1982 as an eight-track recording local punk and pop bands. After a few years he upgraded the studio with a sixteen channel and due to the studio's growing schedule resigned from his job as a draftsman at Stockholm Energy to work full time at the studio.

The chain of events that led to the development of the Swedish Death metal were initiated in 1988 when local teenage band Nihilist asked Skogsberg to record their second demo cassette *Only Shreds Remain*. During the recording sessions the first remnants of the aforementioned 'buzzsaw' sound began to take shape. Nihilist soon morphed into Entombed and with their debut album *Left Hand Path*, the sound was finally refined and crystallised into the Sunlight template. Soon Skogsberg's studio would see an influx of bands wanting to capture the same sound. Bands such as At The Gates, Necrophobic and Darkthrone all came knocking at Skogsberg's studio door. "Some of the bands said to me that, though they wanted a similar sound they didn't want to sound like Entombed," Skogsberg remembers, "I told them that it was not an Entombed sound. It's a sound that came from Sunlight Studios and was the sound I liked".

The grunge-soaked Nineties saw Skogsberg adhering to a hectic recording schedule as the Sunlight Sound became internationally recognised and highly sought out. An array of metal bands filtered through the studio. These included the likes of Grave, Dismember, Necrophobic, and Katatonia to name but a few. In 1993 Skogsberg was again at the helm of Entombed's third album *Wolverine Blues* which, while not straying far from the Sunlight sound, expanded on the studio's sound template, with elements such as hard core punk and hard rock thrown into the aural mix. For Skogsberg this was a marriage of his two favourite styles; rock 'n' roll and punk. Both were successfully fused with death metal creating the genre that Skogsberg calls; 'death and roll'.

Sunlight would finally achieve commercial success on a grand scale when a young band from Stockholm, The Backyard Babies, meshing together glam rock and punk would earn Skogsberg his first two Gold records. The group's second album, 1998's *Total 13* and its 2001 follow-up, the more polished *Making Enemies Is Good* would bring Skogsberg further international acclaim as a go-to producer. But regardless of commercial success, Skogsberg refused to walk the mainstream's paint-by-numbers approach to production. "I don't like mainstream music as it is all down the middle" he says. "I like it on the left side and right side but nothing in the middle. So I am always trying to do some thing in the sound to make it different"

In 2002 Tomas and his family expressed a desire to escape the stress of living and working in Stockholm and decided on a sea change. They moved out to the countryside near Norrtälje, about an hour's drive north of Stockholm. Surrounded by a landscape of dense forest and antiquated roads it provided the idyllic location for a recording studio and so they purchased an old house and began to renovate the late Victorian residence and set up Sunlight Studios in an adjacent barn. Since 2003 bands have made the journey to the studio, and today Skogsberg continues his work there, managing a regular schedule of production, recording sessions and mixing work.

Over the years the Sunlight sound has remained consistent. Skogsberg is sought after not only for his 'sound' but his unique and open-minded approach to recording. While he still records a high quota of death and punk bands, he also occasionally records other styles, something that was instilled in him all those years ago listening to The Beatles and, just like the Fab Four's ground-breaking 1968 album, Skogsberg's studio remains as analogue and old school as he can make it – the only concession to modernity being the addition of a simple computer set-up, but even then Tomas admits "I try to make the computer sound like analogue!"

It was Tomas' open-minded approach to recording other styles and musicians that led me to his studio. With a few days free between shows on my current Swedish tour, the time frame was perfect for me to venture north for a couple days. It is springtime in Sweden and though the temperature is still icy cold, the days are filled with blue skies and sunshine and with the days getting longer, there is less darkness and more daylight, so there is plenty of time to enjoy the journey. It's quite an honour to be recording at this famed studio. In fact, I am informed by Tomas that in all his years here he does not remember any Australian artist having recorded here, so it seems I made some kind of history. It is totally unexpected and I am humbled by the information.

While death metal remains one of the country's internationally recognized genres of music, Sweden is also home to some of the greatest pop music ever made. The most famous of all is Abba who rewrote the pop music rule book. Their 1975 single, 'SOS' is considered by many to be the ultimate pop song. It was the group's defining moment, and in many ways the definitive Abba song. The Who's Pete Townshend described it as "the best pop song ever written". Its sugary-coated surface hides much of the song's inherent musical complexity, and is a study in how to have a successful marriage of ear candy-ness and melodic sophistication. This "marriage", emphasised by the clever melding of moody low-key piano driven verses followed by sweeping acoustic guitar and dramatic multi-layered choruses, shows the arranging skills of both Björn and Benny in the song's effective cocktail of balladry and up-tempo castings. Agnetha's teary and poignant vocal delivery is filled with soulful emotion and heartfelt personality that is underscored with a tinge of aggression, making for one of her best performances on record, and creating for herself the persona of 'queen of heartbreak'.

My experience of the Swedish music scene is one of balancing the yin and yang; the hugely influential death metal scene and the similar influential pop music. I am a sucker for a good melody, one that sticks and never leaves you but I also look for authenticity and a dark edgy in a tune, which is why recording in Sweden fits my music.

Anyway, back to the recording - the following day sees another session in the studio where we added the final touches to the track before the mixing begins in earnest. Recording in new environs like this has certainly influenced the feel and spirit of the track. Being holed up in a studio for any amount of time can sometimes become counter productive, especially in studios located in a city surrounded by distractions but here it has been inspiring, especially as the pace is more laid back and the outside world more attuned to the natural rhythm of the earth.

Working with a world class producer like Tomas enriched my knowledge of recording, giving me a thorough hands-on approach to the process. His expertise and old school mind inspired me in the process. I've recorded in studios before in Australia, and each experience has added to my growing knowledge of recording, which I have utilized when recording and producing my own – or other people's — music but to take oneself out of their comfort zone, travel thousands of miles to another country, over distant lands that are the polar opposite of the spectrum culturally, certainly raises the stakes. My track written in Australia but recorded in Sweden will forever house the spirit of this wonderful land and the experiences it gave me.

With recording done, it was back on the road and the shows. No time for a break or rest. Touring is hard graft at times, and only the strong survive. Touring separates the men from the boys. Bands have imploded on the road. Personalities have fractured. It's tough, but also an adventure. The road less travelled is always more interesting than the well-travelled road by all yet touring is a vital component for any artist. It brings the music to the audience, to the towns, to the country, in real time. It builds the connection with the audience and fans and slowly lays the foundation for the artist to have a long term career. The studio is the stop gap, the place where the music is etched forever and then released to the world. But touring is what keeps everything ticking over. The adventure continues, where it leads nobody knows, but you follow it and you enjoy the ride.

5 - BIG DAY OUT: 2003 - 2007

One of Australia's most popular annual music festivals was the *Big Day Out* which began its life as a one show only event in Sydney in 1992. The following year it expanded to a number of other cities around the country including Melbourne. Based somewhat loosely on the concept behind the American *Lollapalooza* festival, the *Big Day Out* had a successful run until 2014. Held around the tail end of January each year, it was the ideal destination and perfect time for international acts to tour Australia that encompassed performing on the festival bill, basking in the summer sun and enjoying all the spoils the tour brought.

The inaugural *Big Day Out* in 1992 proved to be historic, as it was headlined by Violent Femmes ahead of Nirvana whom at that time were just on the verge of becoming hugely successful on a worldwide scale in the wake of their *Nevermind* album which had only been released a few shorts months earlier. The *Big Day Out* appearance was part of a wider Australian tour being undertaken by the band and with it being the only time Nirvana toured Australia, anyone at those early shows are now the lucky few to have had the privilege of seeing them on Aussie soil. By the time the band had made its way around the country, many venues had to be up-scaled due to the growing interest in the band and its music.

After the lull of the 2002 – 03 holiday season things were beginning to go into overdrive in the industry, as usually around the end of January each year the new releases were beginning to flood journalists' mailboxes. The tail end of January 2003 saw my diary filling up quite quickly, I had several days of nothing but music and interviews in store.

Prior to attending my first *Big Day Out* on Monday, January 27, 2003, I had spent the Sunday evening prior – January 26th – at the Wilco show at the now defunct venue The Palace in St Kilda. The band, led by charismatic front man Jeff Tweedy, were in town for the *Big Day Out* festival and were also performing their own headlining side shows. This was the band's first Australian tour and their most recent studio album at that point was 2001's *Yankee Hotel Foxtrot*. It turned out to be a long night, with the band playing quite an impressive and lengthy show. I left mid-way through the band's second encore in the very early hours of Monday morning, (I was later told the band eventually played a Herculean three hour set) as I had two very hectic days ahead of me, with my schedule overflowing with interviews, the festival and side shows.

The line-up for that year's *Big Day Out* in Melbourne, held at the Royal Melbourne Showgrounds, included acts such as Foo Fighters, Jane's Addiction, Queens of the Stone Age, The Vines, Kraftwerk, Murderdolls, Sparta, The Deftones and Millencolin to name but a few. On the morning of the show before heading out to the festival, I had been scheduled to interview Tom Linton and Jim Adkins from American band Jimmy Eat World, another at 1pm. Being a public holiday that formed part of the Australia Day long weekend, the city's central business district was relatively quiet and the streets bare, a contrast to the usual frantic pace of a normal work day, so finding a parking spot proved relatively easy. I made my way to the hotel, met up with the publicist from Universal Music in the hotel lobby, and made small talk while waiting for the guys to join us. Tom was the first to arrive into the hotel's foyer. Looking well rested and refreshed, he joined us in conversation while we waited for his fellow band mate Jim. Both were in exuberant mood and very much looking forward to their *Big Day Out* set later that day and that same spirit pervaded our interview, which was punctuated by the guys' wicked sense of humour. Touring is an arduous task, and involves much time away from loved ones and family, sometimes many months away. Relationships can become strained and loneliness can set in as personal lives become secondary to the priority of the tour. Touring is one reason why bands implode – it requires not only 'match fitness' but sacrifice and only the strong survive which is made easier if you're blessed with understanding family and friends. In Jim's case, he was recently married and had a child, while Tom was still single. When I asked Tom why that was the case, he told me that he had a girlfriend back home in the US but because of the distance and the constant touring the relationship had ended. Both affirmed that after the *Big Day Out* tour they were going home for a well-deserved and much needed break.

Jimmy Eat World had been badly affected by the tragic events of September 11. The band's most recent album, *Bleed American,* had been released several weeks before 9/11 but the band were forced to change the album's title to simply *Jimmy Eat World*, with the title track renamed 'Salt Sweat Sugar'. After the Jimmy Eat World interview I made my way to the nearest train station and hopped aboard the next train which took me to the Melbourne Showgrounds and I arrived just as Swedish punk rockers Millencolin were finishing their set on the main stage. The festival had two main stages, the *modus operandi* being that while one band played, the other prepared for their set so there would be no break between changeovers in order to keep the flow of the festival and music moving along. The festival also had smaller stages set up where the non-headlining bands performed. I popped into one of the smaller stage areas and caught English alternative rockers The Music ending their set.

As I waited for Jimmy Eat World to come on I noticed Tom Larkin, drummer from Shihad, another band had been forced to rename themselves Pacifier following 9/11! As Jimmy Eat World kicked off the place was overflowing and people roared with excitement. Similar scenes greeted me at the main stage area where Californian rockers Queens of the Stone Age were performing. The crowd of people became a little overpowering, and with the scorching summer sun now making things even hotter, it became very uncomfortable so I made my way to check out Australian punk rockers The Hard Ons play their loud and blistering set at the Triple J stage which was under cover. It was a total contrast to what was happening outside, as surprisingly, their audience was pretty sparse.

Next up I headed out to watch Texan alter-rock outfit Sparta play their set. I really enjoyed them; both the band and music sounded refreshing. After the show the group's lead singer Jim Ward came out to mingle with a wheelchair bound fan. He also took the time out to sign autographs and allow his photo to be taken with a few other fans too. I would be seeing Sparta again when play they played a headlining side show in a more intimate setting at The Corner Hotel the next day.

When the Murderdolls came on their horror-meets-punk-meets-metal styling, inspired largely by the band members love of 1950s cheap horror flicks, Alice Cooper and The Addams Family, wasn't to my taste. Their audience was comprised mainly of younger fans, the type that were also fans of Slipknot which Murderdolls' guitarist Joey Jordison was a full time member of as a drummer. They reminded me too much of Alice Cooper who I'd grown up with, I concluded that I'd seen it all before. I stayed for a couple songs, but afterwards I returned to the main stage area to check out Jane's Addiction who played a great set.

The 1990s alternative rock band from Los Angeles had recently reformed and were enjoying a second wind of success. The band had last toured Australia twelve years before, although Farrell did tour Australia with his other band Porno for Pyros in 1996. Interestingly enough, Farrell is credited with conceiving and debuting the first modern day alternative rock festival, *Lollapalooza*, in the US several months before *Big Day Out's* debut. The band's explosive set displayed how the once drug-fuelled volatility of the band had been replaced by a much leaner and healthier version, and showed a band at the top of their game. A few months later the band released *Strays*, their third studio album and the follow-up to their critically acclaimed *Ritual de lo habitual* from 1990. As Foo Fighters prepared to begin their headlining show I made the decision to leave early in order to avoid the long queues when the festival was over. I eventually saw Foo Fighters play an exceptional show at Rod Laver Arena a few years later but I had another busy day to come the next day with a full schedule of interviews with some of the acts from the festival.

The next day I was kept busy with interviews with the bands. First up was a face-to-face with Erik Ohlsson and Mathias Färm, guitarists from Swedish punk band Millencolin at the Metropole Hotel. Obviously it was a late night for all involved, as upon meeting them they looked like that they had just got out of bed. I saw the band's lead singer and bassist Nikola Sarcevic sitting in the hotel's bistro eating a hearty breakfast with his wife and baby in tow. We took a seat in the outside balcony area, and their grasp of English was very good, thick Swedish accents colouring each word. I took an interest in their tattoos. Having tattoos myself, I asked them about the history of them and they told me they actually got them for free as part of an endorsement deal they had with a tattooist.

Once the Millencolin interview was in the can, I headed for the CBD which was about a few minutes away by car to meet Jim Ward, lead vocalist and guitarist with Texan outfit Sparta. Arriving at the Marriot Hotel, I was greeted by a group of Goths loitering at the entrance, and from the way they were dressed and looked I assumed they were waiting to catch a glimpse of The Murderdolls and The Deftones, who were both staying there. The foyer was a hive of activity with crew, label reps, band members, and hotel guests moving to and fro. A couple of members of nu-metal band The Deftones casually walked past and headed outside. Upon recognizing them the Goth kids went crazy and asked for autographs.

In time the Universal Music publicist arrived and asked me to take a seat inside the hotel's busy café and offered me a drink as Jim Ward was currently in the middle of an interview, I sat and watched the interview while Jim ate a burger and fries before he moved over to where I was sitting, and introduced himself and took a seat. Ward had previously been the founding guitarist of post-hardcore band At The Drive-In which had imploded in early 2001 after they had performed at the 2001 Big Day Out. Ward, along with two of his former At The Drive-In mates Paul Hinojos and Tony Hajjar, formed Sparta soon after. It had been two years since his former band had split, and I knew

Ward was tiring of the constant barrage of questions from media surrounding the circumstances that caused the band's split. I asked him how he felt being constantly asked about the situation. He gave me an honest and heartfelt reply. "There have been years where I wish people didn't talk about it" he admitted before adding, "I think you sort of grow up and learn how to deal with it all and understand why. It is obviously a huge part of my life and it was a great time and part of life. I'm grateful for the opportunity that it afforded me and the experiences I had but I also just consider it the first act of my music. Sometimes I think the perspective gets a little skewed on that band because of the way it ended at such a weird time. So sometimes it gets blown a little out of proportion but that is just me, you know".

I was also curious about what he wanted to achieve with his music. "I think I would like to find that I continue to grow as a writer as my angle has always been to make great songs. That is what I always try to do. I just see all of it as this task and I don't know if I will ever get there, but I just want to write songs and hopefully grow and learn more about orchestration. I'd love to do movie stuff. It is pretty hard to get in to as it is a seriously competitive area of music but I like to continue to chip away at that aspect. I also like to produce more as well so it is a sort of combination of those two things. Obviously, music is going to be the main part of my life as I don't know what else to do". After the interview was done, I thanked him for his time and departed. By this time the remaining members of the band had now gathered at the café, seated themselves and were all digging hungrily into their meals as well.

I quickly jumped into a car and drove to the offices of Roadrunner Records in the suburb of Brunswick. The offices were hidden away in a side street and unless you knew where it actually was, you could have walked past it and not know. Most record labels are like this, usually only discoverable by a small name plate by the front door. At Roadrunner I was scheduled to interview The Murderdolls, who had just released their debut album *Beyond the Valley of the Murderdolls* the previous year. Upon arrival though I was told that only Wednesday 13 (the band's ghoulish looking lead singer) and guitarist Joey Jordison had arrived. I was first introduced to Wednesday 13 who was hanging around the main office. The label's publicist then escorted me downstairs to the quieter surrounds of the building's basement where I was then introduced to Joey, a short fellow dressed from head to toe in black who was sitting alone on a couch in the corner of the room. He came across as extremely shy and softly spoken, a total contrast to his stage persona. In nearly every artist or band I've met I've learned that the more extreme and extrovert the stage persona, the more shy and down to earth they are in real life.

The publicist arrived with some Kentucky Fried Chicken for Joey and he politely asked me if I minded if he ate during the interview, explaining that he'd been so busy with press all morning he'd not had a chance to eat a thing. I said no problem but he quickly changed his mind and said he'd wait. I sensed a bit of tension, so stated before our interview began that I was not going to be asking him about Slipknot. Upon hearing that his attitude changed immediately, he genuinely seemed to appreciate it as he really wanted to focus on The Murderdolls. He told me that all the journalists before me had spent most of their time asking him about Slipknot and not his new band and it was really pissing him off!

In the days leading to Murderdolls arriving in town, the band had been tapped to support The Deftones for two headlining shows in Australia but they had been dropped with no explanation forthcoming. Knowing this was a delicate subject I made a point during the interview to stop the interview, turn off my recorder and ask Joey if I could ask him off the record why The Murderdolls were dropped. He surprisingly replied he was happy to answer my question 'on the record'. I sensed that in my act of turning my recorder off, and having mentioned earlier I had no interest in discussing Slipknot, it demonstrated to him I was a journalist with integrity, one who was not out for a headline or wanting to fuel any sort of rumour or controversy. In turn this made him feel comfortable in my presence and after the interview I thanked him, told him to enjoy his meal and headed home for some dinner myself.

Later that evening I caught Sparta's show at the Corner Hotel in Richmond. The room was packed when they came on at 10:30pm to an enthusiastic crowd. They performed an hour long set which was a bit short in my opinion and it focused heavily on material from their debut album *Wiretap Scars* which had been released about six months earlier. But it was a great show, although very loud, and I really enjoyed the cool interplay between the guitarists.

I became a regular attendee at the *Big Day Out* over the next four years, each January my media AAA pass would be granted and I would spend time backstage hanging with the artists and industry folk and in the crowd watching the bands. However after the 2007 event I lost interest as the line-ups became less interesting and after having attended all the *Big Day Out* festivals since 2003, I felt it was time to move on. While the 2004 event was headlined by Metallica and had bands such as The Darkness, The Strokes and

Kings of Leon on the bill, the 2005 event headlined by Beastie Boys with The Chemical brothers and System Of A Down and others supplementing the bill, was more of a hit and miss affair for me. However the *Big Day Out* of 2006 proved to be one of the best.

A change of location to Princess Park in the inner Melbourne suburb of Carlton from the usual Melbourne Showgrounds facility saw an emphasis more on up and coming bands or "the" bands of 2006 rather than the "big" name acts - such as Metallica - of recent years. The most anticipated act on the line-up was the reformed Stooges. It was the group's first ever tour down under - though James Osterberg, better known as Iggy Pop, had played the *Big Day Out* in 1993. With three members of the original line-up: Iggy and the Asheton brothers (Ron on guitar and Scott on drums) out of the four original members and bassist Mike Watt filling in for the late Dave Alexander who died in 1975 and Steve MacKay providing sax, the band came on just before the sun set and bulldozed their way through the group's first two ground-breaking albums, with tracks interspersed at various points in the set by Pop's solo outing of 2003, *Skull Ring*. In my opinion, and I'm sure others who were there would agree, The Stooges were the stand out band of the festival. Iggy was fifty-eight years old at the time - blonde haired, clad in tight, hipster jeans that exposed his ripped, wrinkled torso but his high-octane showmanship and endless energy which saw him contort, writhe and perform like a primitive man possessed by spirits, he was a show-stopper.

Iggy Pop defined rock 'n' roll's dangerousness by even cutting himself above the right nipple during the performance and jumping into the crowd on several occasions. And then the Godfather of punk invited the audience to jump onstage and join him, which saw a flood of kids, some of them almost forty years his junior, climb up to take up the offer whilst the security went into overdrive, and bringing more than a worrying anxiety attack to the promoters. Unfortunately the headliners who followed them, The White Stripes, were no match for the raw power of Pop and his cohorts. How could any band top an explosive Stooges show? It was a no-win situation.

Australia's very own Deep Purple-Black Sabbath-esque wonder kids Wolfmother proved to be the day's most popular local act, their show a testament to the band's ingenuity, prowess and musicianship which held those in attendance in awe. The band had recently signed a major deal with Capitol Records, so were poised for major international success.

Surprise of the day came in the form of Henry Rollins' spoken word set which proved very popular amid the hammering sounds of the nearby tents. His anecdotes regarding Iggy Pop, The Ramones – particularly his moving experience with Johnny Ramone on his death bed – and his recalling of his first visit to the *Big Day Out* back in '92 were laced with his outspoken political commentary and views on the current state of world affairs. All in all, with capacity crowds of around 39,000 under a very hot sun, and much jovial spirit around and the wiff of the sweet leaf at times permeating the air, the *Big Day Out* of 2006 was a memorable event.

The following year's festival continued the fine tradition, with an abundance of local acts such as The Vines and JET who had made it big overseas in recent years, the highpoint of the festival. JET, who had played on one of the smaller side stages at the 2004 event, proudly flew the flag for Aussie rock both musically and literally and their *Big Day Out* performance was a homecoming on the huge main stage. The very first time I saw JET perform was at an outside Christmas party in 2002 when the band had just signed a deal with US major Elektra Records. They performed a special invite-only performance at a Melbourne street press magazine I was writing for at the time so I got to know the boys fairly well. They had just released an EP called *Dirty Sweet* so played tracks from that and gave all in attendance a taster of what was to come.

I recall a lazy Saturday afternoon in early 2003 spent at a local watering hole in Melbourne with the band, their manager and a handful of close family and friends, at a farewell party as they were preparing to depart for Los Angeles to record their debut album *Get Born*. While relaxing in the hotel's lounge area with drinks in hand and talking to JET's manager, our conversation was suddenly interrupted by a phone call. Excusing himself he took the call, and then after he had finished, turned around to me and said, 'That was The Rolling Stones, and they've asked if JET could be their support band on their upcoming Australian leg of their 2003 Australian tour'. The band would fly back from the US just two weeks into recording sessions to do the support shows that February.

So by the time of JET's Big Day Out set in 2006 all that touring had made them a very tight hard-rocking unit, having said that, occasionally the band did suffer from some tempo misfires. Lead singer and guitarist Nic Cester looked the part of a rock star, with the scarf, jacket, tight jeans and aviator sunglasses, he oozed cool. During their performance someone in the crowd threw a bottle of water at Drummer Chris Cester that luckily narrowly missed him. I later heard somebody did the same thing to him at the Sydney *Big Day Out*. Was it the tall poppy syndrome rearing its ugly head?

I spent a portion of my day in the VIP tent where a number of artists and their camps hung out with a few drinks to relax before or after a show or just to mingle with industry folks. Nic Cester walked in prior to performing JET's set so he and I caught up for a quick chat. The day was back dropped by great weather not too hot and not too cold, though standing in the sun the warmth was certainly penetrating your skin. As for the sound, it wasn't the best due to the swirling wind but that was the only disappointing thing to the whole day.

6 - WHEN ROCK STARS BEHAVE BADLY

Being a successful recording artist usually comes with its own inherent pressures and the bigger the star, the more pressure they tend to be under. The pressure to keep record sales on an upward trend, to conform to record company demands, to maintain the endless record and tour cycle, and on top of that to constantly keep oneself evolving as artist can lead to very public breakdowns. The public is usually oblivious to the pressures artists are subjected to, to the extent that when an artist unexpectedly suffers a meltdown in the public eye, it makes for tabloid headlines. Sometimes the meltdown will occur in concert or at a press conference or in front of a fan or group of fans. Some artists who had the courage to change tack in their career will suffer a backlash from critics and fans alike.

For Smashing Pumpkins' Billy Corgan it was the latter that led him to having a meltdown whilst on stage in Melbourne in 2005 which I witnessed. Corgan has always done things his own way. Highly driven and obsessive to the point of perfection, he tends to prefer the route less travelled. His whole career attests to this fact; starting with The Smashing Pumpkins, a band he formed in 1988 with guitarist James Iha, which fused his love for heavy guitars and pop melodies sprinkled with flourishes of psychedelia, his ambitious drive steered the band to their critical and commercial zenith via their 1995 magnum opus *Mellon Collie and the Infinite Sadness*. Having finally reached the top of the mountain, as well as having become a musical focal point for disenfranchised youth, Corgan and his cohorts took an unexpected left turn on their next album, 1998's *Adore*, which was awash with electronic elements which echoed Corgan's later solo work. The aftermath of the commercial success and the inherent pressures caused the band's internal relationships to fracture, so much so that by the time of *Adore* those relationships were in disarray. In 2000 the band officially split (though they reformed in 2006 with a modified line-up and as of 2021 were still an ongoing concern) so Corgan embarked on a solo career.

Prior to arriving in Australia for his solo tour in July 2005 Corgan had tried his hand with another band, Zwan, which fell apart due to interpersonal relationships yet again and less than a year after releasing an album, 2003's *Mary Star of the Sea* which was soaked heavily in quasi-religious symbolism, he returned as a solo artist and had just released his debut *The Future Embrace* which featured electronic beats and synth-driven songs that was musically poles apart from the halcyon days of The Smashing Pumpkins and poorly received.

It was in support of this album that Corgan undertook an Australian tour in July 2005. His last appearance in Australia had been in 1998 with The Smashing Pumpkins. I caught his show in the confines of the old world architecture of the historic Palais Theatre in bay side St.Kilda. Like many others who were there on the night, we all expected his new album to get an airing and presumed he would at least be playing a few songs from the Pumpkins catalogue. We were all in for a shock in that department, and not in regards to the Pumpkin songs, but more so to the reaction from sections of the audience and Corgan's response.

Taking to a minimalist stage and backed by three other musicians, it was more akin to going to a nightclub and listening to a DJ spin some CDs than a live concert. Now I will give credit where it is due, Corgan performed the album very well, with his mix of Depeche Mode meets Cure excursions but on that evening he seemed to lack any kind of stage presence. Standing over six feet tall, the bald Corgan was a towering figure on stage, with just himself and a guitar in hand, but that night he lacked energy and spark. It was as though he was just going through the motions. Maybe it was due to the audience response, as many remained seated for the first batch of songs or maybe it was the poor ticket sales he had received for his show.

The only moment in the show where the energy level changed was when Corgan performed a twisted cover of AC/DC's 'Long Way To The Top', which with its electronic beats and monotone vocalizing that would make the legendary Bon Scott turn in his grave. But the unexpected surprise of the whole evening was at the end of the show when fans started shouting out for Corgan to play some Pumpkin songs. It was obvious that he was feeling the heat and as the calls continued, it began to get to him. At one point he asked the audience if he could "live my life for today" but that didn't placate the audience. In fact the fans soon started to turn on each other with one section calling out for some "rock music" and "Pumpkins" only to be countered by the opposing group's hisses and boos. Whatever, it seemed Corgan's legacy with his former band greatly outweighed that of his solo standing.

Then it all sadly turned sour; after the calls of "Pumpkins! Pumpkins!" slowly increased in volume, Corgan's frustration and exasperation finally boiled over. He threw his microphone stand down, turned around and walked off stage. Show over! Most of the crowd were shell shocked, though it was a very confusing situation. Just the previous month on the day of the US release of his solo album *The Future Embrace*, Corgan had taken out a full page ad in *The Chicago Tribune* in which he proclaimed that he wanted his band back. It seemed that the pressures of the past few years and the disinterest from the critics and fans of his solo outing and lacklustre sales, Corgan would release two more solo albums, under the name of William Patrick Corgan, 2017's *Ogilala* and 2019's *Cotillions*, though both were in the acoustic realm rather than electronica. At the end of the day Corgan's unfortunate meltdown served to illustrate that stars of his ilk are, like all of us, complex human beings - we all face problems in our daily lives and even rock stars can succumb to pressure. The difference being that many of us do it in private or among friends and family while stars, whose lives are lived in the public eye, have the added glare of the Joe Public with which to contend.

While the pressures can lead some to a meltdown, for others the rigours of public life and their relationship with fellow band members, the media and even the fans themselves can bring out the worst in them. An example of this type of situation occurred when The Saints' Chris Bailey was in town a few months after Corgan's tour. Bailey was co-founder and vocalist for Australian punk rockers The Saints, formed in 1973. The Saints took their inspiration from the early rumblings of Detroit's garage rock scene that from the mid-1960s with bands such as The Stooges and MC5 – the unique sounds of these bands soon permeated across the Pacific and metamorphosed into an epochal musical force in the hands of The Saints who went on to become entangled with the British punk-rock scene starting in 1976. Although the Australian scene may have been closely related to its British counterpart, the results that emanated from it were very different. The Saints opted for a rawer and wilder style of The Stooges and MC5 rather than Sex Pistol's primal assault.

The Saints' debut single '(I'm) Stranded' pre-dated the debut singles of The Damned, Sex Pistols, Buzzcocks, The Clash and all their UK punk contemporaries. When '(I'm) Stranded' appeared in September on the band's own Fatal Records, it was all but ignored by the Australian music industry but the band sent out a copy to UK's *Sounds* magazine – then championing the punk revolution - who ended up reviewing it as 'Single of this and EVERY week'. Immediately in its wake the UK branch of EMI ordered EMI Australia to sign the band after they had originally passed. The Saints quickly packed their bags and headed for the UK for an inaugural UK tour that saw The Saints opening for Talking Heads and The Ramones.

Playing venues such as London's Roundhouse and Manchester's Electric Circus, the band found it a bit of a culture shock. "In Oz we hadn't done that much gigging so the audience we were used to was very mixed, like there were females in the audience as well," remembers Chris Bailey, "but on that first tour of the UK, because of all that 'punky' nonsense that was happening, it was kind of like playing at the YMCA with an audience that was predominantly male and draped in the fashions of the day. Coming from Oz it was a little bit like 'where are the women?' It took us a few years before we started getting any girls in the audience. That whole fashion thing was secondary to us and we weren't known for our sartorial elegance or fashion contribution. Most English and American bands associate a look with the music, but to us that was totally irrelevant".

"The Saints were ahead of the English fashion scene"

concurs Saints co-founder and guitarist Ed Kuepper, "but we just weren't acknowledged as such by the press. There wasn't a scene in Australia to really compare anything to."

"And we didn't really mix with any of the other punk bands," Bailey continues, "I guess because we were signed to a big label there was a bit of hype around us. I guess we got invited to the right parties for awhile. I found that coming from Oz, where we weren't terribly well known, we had our own little gang when we played gigs there. And the gigs didn't have a lot of people so it was kind of a more approachable, friendlier scene but when we got to the UK it was all very business orientated."

"Like I thought Sex Pistols were funny rather than trailblazing. I remember the first time I heard the Sex Pistols I thought they were the [Sensational] Alex Harvey Band with a Cockney singer. The Sex Pistols were kind of like The Monkees with a great marketing twist. The one distinction, which I think is still there is in the UK, music is much more closely associated to fashion than status whereas in Oz it's quite possible to meet some bloke from some band and it doesn't matter what kind of music it is, you've got music in common."

The fact that punk had become a thriving business for the record labels would turn out to be a portent of what was to come, as The Saints found out when it came to album number two. "When we weren't able to replicate the first album and wanted to be a bit more adventurous on the second," explains Bailey, "that didn't go down terribly well with the label. You see the first record was done in a weekend and was virtually the live set with some guitar overdubs but when we got to the second album we had a budget of £10,000 or £12,000 and had the choice to work with some fabulous engineers. Then just before the third album it started to go pear-shaped. We all knew EMI was going to drop the contract and management had already decided to leave. We were just contractually allowed to do that record. On top of that, I had already started thinking about putting together a new band."

With Drummer Ivor Hay and Kuepper now having departed, Bailey moved forward with a new line-up which continued to change over the ensuing years, with Bailey remaining the band's sole leader and driving force. In 1986 the band returned with a more refined sound and finally achieve their commercial breakthrough with *All Fool's Day*, the band's seventh studio outing.

I had spoken to Bailey 18 months prior to arriving in Australia late one night for an interview later published *Total Guitar* magazine in the UK. That interview was undertaken in order to tie in with the soon to be released *All Times Through Paradise* 4-CD set. Bailey was known for his arrogance and distaste for the media and music journalists in particular but our interview seemed to go well and we spoke at length. But then again, he was in Amsterdam at the time of the call, so perhaps the environmental surrounds played a big part on his "happier than normal" persona.

When I found out Bailey was due to do a solo tour of Australia and having heard that he was pleased with my original piece, his management organized a meet and greet with him when he came through Melbourne. I had already been warned by my journo friends that Bailey was disliked by the Australian media due to his arrogance and egocentricity. I also was told by a publicist that he was 'difficult'. On the evening of the meeting, I was informed that his management in the UK had been trying to get hold of Bailey for days without much luck but they confirmed that Bailey knew about our meeting and we would be able to get together as he had already okayed it. I arrived at the Northcote Social Club in inner north Melbourne and walked into a dimly lit, alcohol-soaked band room at the back. I asked one of the crew who were setting up equipment where I could find Bailey and he pointed me in his direction. I caught a glimpse of the man and went up and introduced myself since he was expecting me. To my surprise all he managed was a quick hand shake which was underscored by a just as quick 'hi' under his breath before he walked off with another person and left me to it.

He seemed to be inebriated and possibly a little stoned. I had never experienced this type of reaction before from any artist I had met or interviewed before. I never saw him again until he hit the stage for his show later that evening. His stage performance seemed to further underscore his inebriated state. Taking swigs from a wine bottle between songs, his show degenerated into a chaotic mess. At one point he became antagonistic towards the audience and, remembering what had happened only a few months earlier at the Corgan show, and sensing that things would only deteriorate from there, I decided it was the best to make my exit and depart midway through his set. Needless to say I never got that interview!

Going from obscurity to mass popularity in such a short time can bring its own pressures, especially when the way it comes about in the most unlikely way. In 2003 American indie-rockers Death Cab For Cutie were invited by Australian band Something For Kate to tour Australia for the very first time. Back then the quartet were relatively unknown to Australian audiences outside of the indie music circle. When the band returned for their next Australian tour in 2006 their profile had risen considerably, having broken into the mainstream with their record sales having now surpassed the million units mark following the use of their songs on American TV teen drama series *The O.C.* which aired from 2003 to 2007. Death Cab For Cutie's music not only featured in the series but they were also written into the fictional narrative. In the interim they had signed to a major record label, Atlantic (in the USA) and Warners (in Australia), and had their songs featured on the soundtracks of other popular TV shows such as *Six Feet Under* and *Californication*.

In July 2006 I was scheduled to interview the band who were in town as part of a worldwide tour in support of their major label debut album *Plans* which had been released the year prior. They were due to perform a show later that evening at Melbourne's famed Forum, the show itself had been sold out for about three months. I arrived at the Medina Hotel, only a couple of minutes walking distance from The Forum, and waited in the foyer with the band's label rep while the band undertook sound checking something that eventually went over time.

After sound check a couple of the band members, including singer Ben Gibbard, arrived and quickly headed to the elevator to go to one of upper floors where their allocated rooms were. Having only arrived in Melbourne earlier that day, and having just wrapped up their sound check, I assumed jet lag had well and truly set in so the band needed to catch up on some sleep before their show later that evening. With no sighting of the band's guitarist, engineer and producer Chris Walla, who I was to interview there and then, the band's record label representative called their tour manager over to us to remind him that Walla had an interview scheduled with me. The tour manager mentioned that he had tried to call Chris but claimed that due to the jet lag, it seemed he had forgotten about the interview.

Strangely enough, and contradicting his previous statement, he further explained to us that straight after sound check Chris had told him he was off to check another band play but would return in time for the band's in-store appearance which was scheduled before their show began. He had also turned off his cell phone. The in-store was due to start in about an hour's time too – we'd already been waiting for about an hour or so by then – and so he suggested maybe we could do the interview just prior to the show or possibly after the show.

Unfortunately, due to the fact I had to head out to perform my own show on the other side of town, this would not be possible. And with Death Cab For Cutie heading up to Sydney for another show the following evening, there would be no other time available where the interview could take place. Faced with this scenario we agreed on rescheduling a phone interview sometime in the following week. The tour manager apologized for Chris Walla's no show.

When the phone interview with Walla finally happened a week later, I brought up the matter of his absence at our previously scheduled face to face interview the week prior to his attention. Strangely enough he insisted he didn't know anything about it, again contradicting everything we had been told previously, and said it could be blamed on the jet lag. I sensed something wasn't right, and that Walla was not being totally upfront. What led me to conclude this was the fact that about an hour before the phone interview I had received a call from the band's publicist strongly advising me that the band's tour manager had requested that no questions relating to the television show *The O.C* were to be asked due to the amount of questions thus far from journalists in earlier interviews that repeatedly kept asking about the band relationship with the TV series which had made them famous. It seemed the band weren't too enamoured that their route to fame via the television series as it took away from their indie street cred which led to them dismissing any discussion of the subject and, in Walla's case, avoiding a face to face interview.

I would get another chance to meet up with the band again three years later in February 2009 when they were touring their sixth album *Narrow Stairs*. On the day of my interview they were again playing The Forum Theatre later that evening which had sold-out for two nights. After their Melbourne shows they were scheduled to fly to Sydney for the next stop of their Australian tour.

Having arrived at The Quest, I walked into the foyer and past a couple guys waiting in the hallway. Unrecognisable from the clothes they wore, the only tell-tale sign were their thick American accents. I again connected with the band's record label publicist who greeted me upon entry into the foyer. The hotel was the location of the interview with Chris Walla again scheduled for late afternoon. The publicist and I chatted for a while but thoughts of the 2006 scenario ran through my mind again as Walla was still yet to arrive.

Finally word came through that we needed to make our way to one of the top floors and as we entered the room which had been set up for the interviews, it was a flurry of activity. I was allocated the bedroom as another interview was being filmed with Nick Harmer (Bassist) and Jason McGerr (Drummer), who I recognised were the guys I had walked past earlier in the hotel lobby. The same tour manager was there again. We made small talk before, to my great relief, Walla finally arrived for his interview.

I was finally introduced to Walla and we sat down. He quickly opened the side window of the room to let some fresh air in and sat on the bed while I sat on a chair and conducted the interview.

He was quietly spoken and looked almost geeky and fragile in stature. I again brought up the subject of our last encounter back in 2006 where he never turned up and where we had to reschedule a phone interview. He remembered speaking to me and admitted to actually seeing the interview later online. This was a different Walla to the one I had spoken to previously. Maybe he and the band had come to accept their unorthodox route to success, or maybe it was due to the fact he had finally released a solo album *Field Manual* the year before and was able to express himself musically which may not have been possible through Death Cab For Cutie. He was enthused about the topics discussed unlike the previous occasion. We ended up having an enjoyable 20 minute chat. He informed me he was going to his room on level 2. He told me he needed to go buy some clothes as all his clothes had been left behind in Adelaide at the previous night's show and so he needed to have a change of clothes. He mentioned that the band was leaving Melbourne early Wednesday morning, and that he loved being in the city and had friends there too. Once they left Australia they were due to commence the next leg of their tour in the US that April. My impression of him changed that day.

When the news came out in 2014 that Walla had left the band after 17 years and moved to Norway, everything that happened on those two previous encounters I had with him years earlier, regarding his attitude and no-show, came into focus a lot better. Looking back there were cryptic signs along the way, maybe not intentional on Walla's part, but certainly sub-conscious. For example Death Cab For Cutie's eighth record, 2015's *Kintsugi*, which was the last album Walla contributed to as a fully paid up member of the band and released after his departure, took its name from the Japanese art form of mending yet highlighting the broken parts and its repair process as part of the object's history. In hindsight that title made perfect sense as to what was going on internally within the band's ranks that led to Walla's exit.

In several interviews Gibbard gave after Walla's departure he revealed the relationship between the two was "complicated" and in one of my interviews with Walla, he at one point said, "Everything tends to have a really natural evolution and a linear flow to it". He also had revealed to me that he was very keen to make a pop record. "I don't know what it is" he said before adding, "my pendulum swings pretty wide I guess", which really summed up my whole experience with Chris Walla.

7 - COME UP AND SEE ME

It is an hour after sunrise in late January 2012 as I get up and stroll into the kitchen to make myself a coffee. The peace and quiet of the morning is soon interrupted by the loud ringing of my phone. I pick up and the voice of a well-spoken Londoner is instantly recognizable. It is British singer/songwriter Steve Harley calling from his Georgian home in Suffolk, England.

"Good morning Joe, it's Steve Harley here. Just to let you know I'm finally coming to Australia! It's going to be around March/April and it will be a promo tour so I wanted to discuss the plans with you and to invite you to accompany me as my official guitar player on the tour and also to ask you if you could be my chauffeur?"

"That would be an honour and a total pleasure" I replied.

"Wonderful to hear".

For Steve Harley that Australian tour had taken him thirty-nine years to finally come to fruition, as it was back in 1975 when Steve's biggest hit in Australia and his signature song known worldwide, and a UK number 1, 'Make Me Smile (Come Up And See Me)', peaked at number 17 on the Australian music charts. Though Steve went on to have further hits elsewhere, in Australia, that's the tune he's remembered by. I first purchased that song as part of a compilation album on vinyl called *Explosive Hits '75*. I was ten at the time and just could not get enough of that song: the flamenco-styled acoustic guitar solo was hugely melodic, and I would air guitar to it regularly. Who would have known that almost forty years later I would be playing that song and solo with the man himself? Life is certainly full of surprises.

Born Stephen Nice in South-east London in 1951 at the peak of the world polio epidemic, Steve would succumb to the disease at the age of three and was in and out of hospital until he was sixteen. He was one of the lucky ones, a survivor, escaping with nothing worse than atrophy in one leg. While recuperating in hospital during one of his later stays in his teens, he began reading classic books by D.H Lawrence, Hemingway and Steinbeck which kindled his interest in words. As a 12-year-old, during a long-term hospital stay, he discovered the music of Bob Dylan which ignited his interest in music. In his late teens he pursued his ambition of becoming a reporter. He spent three years in journalism with stints on local newspapers in Essex before taking up a position at the *East London Advertiser* but his morality got the better of him when one day his editor demanded Harley report the story of a female shoplifter who had absent-mindedly walked out of her local supermarket with a couple of cans of soup. Harley strongly opposed the writing of the story as he believed it was unfair to label her a thief. This caused him to become so disillusioned with the reporting business that he stopped wearing his tie and grew his hair long, which resulted in him being fired. Now free to pursue his growing passion for music, he took his acoustic guitar and began busking around London in 1972, and at the same time changed his surname from Nice to the more stage friendly Harley. He would road test songs he had written in front of passing audiences in subways and public areas such as Hyde Park Corner and Marble Arch.

Steve soon formed Cockney Rebel and having

performed just five shows the band signed a three-album deal with EMI. Together they went on to have six hit singles between 1974 and 1976 before Steve pursued a solo career with his debut album *Hobo with a Grin* surfacing in 1978.

Steve eventually relocated to the United States in the late 1970s and told me that his year-long sojourn in the US was spent in a haze of drug-fuelled partying and enjoying the spoils that came from being a successful rock star. This proved detrimental to staying focused on his burgeoning solo career, so he made the decision to return to London. It was while he was on a promotional visit flying from Glasgow to Newcastle in 1979 that he met his wife Dorothy, a Scottish air stewardess. They eventually married and he left his hedonistic lifestyle behind for good. The couple clocked up forty years of marriage in 2020.

The Eighties saw Steve take a long sabbatical away from the music industry to focus on raising a family. In the meantime he scored a major role in the stage musical *Phantom of The Opera* but at the eleventh hour was unceremoniously replaced by Michael Crawford. Steve accepted this ousting philosophically and just "got up and got on" with his career. Ironically in 1986, he garnered a Top 10 hit with Sarah Brightman with the title song from *Phantom Of The Opera*.

He returned to a hectic schedule of recording and touring in the 1990s and later reformed Cockney Rebel, albeit with a revamped line-up and released *The Quality of Mercy* album in 2005. He also embarked on a stint as a radio presenter from 1999 until 2008 as host of BBC Radio 2's *Sounds Of The Seventies* programme. He released his next solo album *Stranger Comes to Town* in 2010 which would be the album he would promote on his inaugural Australian visit.

I had first connected with Steve via my work as a music journalist in the early 2000s. I did a number of phone interviews with him over the years that were published in various music magazines as well as a major cover story for UK magazine *Acoustic*. We shared a background in journalism and built a good rapport and stayed in touch. Early on I had mentioned to Steve I was a musician and so he asked me if I had any music to send him, after he'd listened to it he told me how much he liked my guitar playing. Steve had expressed a desire to finally tour Australia as it was the only country he had never toured as he was doing about 100 shows all over Europe.

In August 2006 he called me and said he was coming for a show at the Sydney Opera House in November of that year as he had received an invitation from fellow British music artist John Otway. The eccentric Otway had put together plans to charter his own plane, bringing along 350 fans who had paid to be part of his trip around the world. Otway would be filming his adventure and Steve was hoping to have his 45 minute set at Australia's famed Sydney Opera House filmed so that it could be released on DVD at some point in the future.

It would be perfect timing for Steve as he had a 3–CD anthology set coming out in early October of that year – *The Cockney Rebel - A Steve Harley Anthology*. Unfortunately that tour never happened as Otway cancelled it a few months out and enquiries I later made to the Opera House confirmed that there was no booking nor any mention of a scheduled Otway show at the Opera House. It was a very strange set of events.

When I visited the UK for the first time in late 2009 Steve invited me to meet up with him and hang out. But upon arrival in London Steve called and informed me that he was holed up in the studio recording a new album *Stranger Comes to Town* released in 2010, and so was unable to meet. He apologized profusely as he was very much looking forward it. Being a musician I totally understood his situation. So it would be another three years before we finally got to meet.

Anyway, back to that January phone call – Steve gave me a list of songs he wanted me to learn so I could play with him and I spent the ensuing months learning all the required material plus more. Eventually the promo tour was set in stone and promotion began. The plan was to generate interest via numerous media appearances, live acoustic sessions, as well as meet with interested promoters for a possible full blown 2013 Australian tour.

So on Tuesday April 10, 2012, a couple days after Easter, Steve finally arrived at Melbourne airport on a 5.45am flight from London. Upon arrival he called me to let me know of his safe arrival. He told me he was feeling good and had got some good sleep on the plane, though he did mention that come the afternoon he may feel differently once jet lag set in. I informed him he could expect me at his hotel around mid-afternoon.

My morning was spent packing my bags and organizing a hire car I would be using for the entire duration of his visit, as well as picking up an acoustic guitar I had organized for Steve to use for the duration of his visit too. Local guitar manufacturer Maton had kindly offered to loan Steve one of their dreadnought acoustics.

Come mid-afternoon I finally arrived at the Hilton On The Park, a plush inner city hotel where Steve was staying. It had just gone 2.45pm as I made my way to one of the rooms located at the top floor of the hotel. As I approached Steve's room and was about to knock, there was a "Do Not

Disturb" sign on the handle. As Steve was expecting me, I gently tapped on the door, as Steve greeted me with a hug we were both thrilled to finally meet after so long, and he mentioned how the jet-lag was finally kicking in. I placed his loaned guitar and my own guitar on the floor beside his bed. We planned to rehearse the songs in his room.

He offered me a coffee and we chatted for a while. He grabbed his acoustic to get a feel of it and really liked how it sounded and felt. I picked up my guitar and started strumming some chords, and Steve mentioned how it had a slightly richer and deeper tone to it. Then we casually ran through the songs that Steve had given me to learn, the songs that we were going to perform at the acoustic sessions. He asked if we could start with 'Make Me Smile (Come Up And See Me)'. In some ways this was my audition as this was the very first time Steve and I had actually played together. Since I had already spent the months leading up to this learning the tune I was confident with any of the songs Steve had asked me to learn, I was very relaxed rather than feeling any sense of nervousness for my big audition moment. So we played the song and I played the recognizable guitar solo, after which he exclaimed, "you did learn it (the solo), well done!" My audition was a success and you could say I got the job. As we ran through it I improvised some backing vocals which he later said he really liked and requested I keep them in.

Steve later told me stories of how over the years many other guitarists had played the solo but only a few had performed it correctly. Obviously the original guitarist Jim Cregan was one of them, along with a couple of others he had worked with over the years and he added my name to the list. I felt it was an honour to have Steve's seal of approval.

The next song we ran through was 'A Friend For Life'. Funnily, when we got to the middle eight, he seemingly played the wrong chord. I tried following his lead in order to salvage the error, but told him, "It's the wrong chord". He admitted his mistake and said that the jet lag had started to affect him. He also added that he was also hearing my guitar parts that I was playing in his head, so complimented me further on my lead work.

It was a relaxing atmosphere as we sat, me on his bed and he on the chair near the window overlooking the scenic view of the city's Fitzroy Gardens below. Next we ran through 'The Last Time I Saw You' followed by 'Journey's End', where I improvised a guitar solo, which again he complimented. I also improvised a melody line adding it to the ending part of the song, which he seemed to really like as he asked me to keep it in.

The songs we rehearsed were to form a six-song, thirty-minute set to be played at a lunch time session in a city record store later that week, but we later got word that it had been cancelled. After the impromptu rehearsal we chatted further about family, career and more, before he told me that the jet lag was beginning to kick in and he really needed to get some sleep. He asked me if I didn't mind taking him to get a bottle of locally produced white wine to help him unwind. So I drove him to a nearby convenience store then dropped him back at the hotel. As he got out of the car I asked him what sort of dress code he wanted me to adhere to for the TV and radio performances the next day and he replied, "...you wear a bandanna, right? I like that, as I want you to be you, so wear it, as it's your image".

The next day I was back at his hotel to pick him up so we could make our way to the scheduled live acoustic performances. Steve told me he never liked to be late for an appointment so wanted to make sure we got there nice and early at every media outlet. As we drove off he said he needed some new shoes, something comfortable for him to wear, so I drove him to Smith Street, home to several shoe factory outlets such as Converse and Nike in search of some Reeboks. Smith Street in Melbourne's inner north with its grit-meets-chic appeal has a chequered past. As one of the oldest thoroughfares in the city, it is now home to a diverse range of retail, arty and cuisine offerings, it's a must visit on many touring artists' schedules when in town. In the early 2000s folk legend Bob Dylan, while in-between shows on Australian tour and trying to remain incognito, strolled around the street for a few hours to savour its delights. Unable to find anything suitable, Steve eventually bought a pair of Adidas runners instead. With shopping done, we made our way over to South Melbourne to Noise 11, a well-known music website that filmed many interviews and live performances of visiting touring artists for their popular website. Steve and I were scheduled for a 2pm acoustic performance and interview that was to be filmed. Since we arrived in ample time, and with glorious weather, we took a seat outside a nearby pub, enjoyed a social drink and chatted further while we waited before heading to the studios only a few doors down.

At the studio Steve asked for a cup of tea, after which we both set up under the lights and positioned ourselves in front of the cameras. Once we were comfortable the interview began in earnest. It was a lengthy interview about 45 minutes, and once it was over it was time for us to perform two songs, 'Journey's End' and 'Make Me Smile (Come Up And See Me)' which were filmed. I did a quick tuning check of both of our guitars. Just before the camera rolled Steve asked the host and camera person to make sure I was credited in the final edit with my name clearly present. After we had performed the songs photos were taken and then it was time to move on to our next interview and another performance, this time at a local community radio station in Mentone located south of the city. As time was slipping by, and since it would be a 30 minute drive with rush hour nearing, we jumped in the car and hit the road.

We arrived at our next destination, Southern FM situated in Bayside, with minutes to spare, so we quickly rushed in, seated ourselves and prepared for the acoustic session, which was to be recorded for broadcast at a later date. This time we performed three numbers; 'Journey's End', 'A Friend For Life' and 'Make Me Smile (Come Up And See Me)'. In my opinion, this particular performance of 'Make Me Smile (Come Up And See Me)' turned out to be our best yet. It was a more confident and strident affair, as we were finally getting into the groove of things. Once we strummed the final chord of the song, Steve turned to me and gave me a wink of approval. With the set now done Steve was escorted into the adjourning studio to do his live-to-air interview for another show which was airing on the same radio station. During the hour he was in there I watched proceedings from the side.

It had been a long day, so fatigue was starting to set in for both of us and as 6pm came and went we made our way back to Steve's hotel. By the time we had navigated our way through the busy evening traffic and I had dropped Steve off, it had gone 8pm, and since I had not had anything to eat since breakfast, I was looking forward to getting home for dinner.

Thursday was our scheduled in-store but it was

cancelled at the last minute so it left for only one media engagement for Steve. I escorted him to the interview in the afternoon, and later that evening we shared a wonderful evening having dinner together at a restaurant that was walking distance from his hotel. Steve shared many war stories, particularly tales about his friendships with David Bowie and Marc Bolan. Steve spent a lot of time at Bolan's house during the final eighteen months of his life before he was tragically killed in a car accident in September 1977. Even today when Steve talks about his late friend he speaks with a voice that is tinged with sadness. Steve recalled the time when Marc told him that he had sold a certain amount of singles that week on the chart but, as they shared the same record label at the time Steve knew very well the correct figure, as Bolan had a tendency to exaggerate his accomplishments, particularly when it came to sales figures by adding another zero!

There was another early start the next morning as we had a full schedule of radio interviews and performances. First up was a major interview Steve was confirmed to do with an Australian commercial radio network. As I drove to the hotel entrance, Steve was waiting patiently in the foyer for me. He gets into the car, and greets me with 'Happy Birthday Joe!' (It was my birthday) and we made our journey to the radio station on the other side of town. The interview was a pre-record so it would be airing in a few days. I waited outside the transparent glass wall while Steve did his interview. In the afternoon we drove to another radio station for another pre-record interview and acoustic performance. We entered the building, got into the lift to take us to one of the upper floors, and once we arrived in the foyer, we were instructed to wait for the DJ to meet us. Steve asked the receptionist for a cup of tea. A few minutes later the DJ surfaced and after introductions all around, we were ushered into the studio. The DJ seemed surprised that we had brought along our guitars, so with curiosity getting the better of him, asked us what the guitars were for?

"Because we've been instructed by our publicist there was going to be a performance of 'Make Me Smile' as well" I informed him. Apparently he knew nothing about it, but he seemed overjoyed at the suggestion. He quickly rushed out to the sound engineer and brought him into the studio to set everything up for the performance. So as the sound engineer set up the mics and video for recording, Steve went into an adjoining studio to do the interview.

It was a very casual affair as the DJ explained he would be editing it later into a more cohesive interview, then we moved into the studio where the acoustic performance would be taking place. I quickly checked the guitars tunings and we took our seats. The DJ and another radio person who now had entered the room, took a front row seat on the floor and watched us perform 'Make Me Smile (Come Up And See Me)'. We did a brief sound check and the sound engineer gave us the go-ahead, and off we went. Just before starting the song proper Steve explained the background to it and then played a bit of the song in the way it was originally written and demo-ed, which was much slower and with a bluesier feel than to the final recorded version. Again we did it in a single take. If it's a pre-record sometimes artists will play a song a number of times and pick the best take, but for us, we were now in such a tight groove that a single take captured it all. The session was also filmed and later uploaded to the station's website and after a few quick photos it was time to go. We were advised that the interview and performance would be aired during drive time the following Monday. As we were heading back to hotel, Steve surprised me by saying he'd like to take my wife and I out for dinner to celebrate my birthday and requested I choose a nice restaurant and whatever food I liked and book a table for three for later that evening.

Later that night we picked Steve up from his hotel and took him to an Italian restaurant I had booked. I introduced my wife Liz who was waiting for us outside. We took our seats in the guest area and I had the time of my life. We stayed for about four hours. Steve surprised me with a birthday cake made of ice cream that had a candle on top, which he had organized earlier with the maître d. He then sang Happy Birthday to me! As it was nearing midnight, we made our way back to Steve's hotel said good night, and my wife and I headed home. It was a birthday I'll never forget.

After a busy week, Steve spent the weekend relaxing and exploring the delights of Melbourne, doing much walking through the nearby parks and gardens, enjoying the Melbourne Autumn sunshine – Saturday was a very mild 25c – and visiting the art galleries and indulging his passion for horse racing by reading the form guide. He also watched the races on his laptop as he sat around the hotel pool. I caught up with him again on Monday and took him to beach side St Kilda where he was scheduled to do a guest appearance on a popular Australian TV show that combined a quiz element and live music performances before a live studio audience. Steve would be performing his signature tune with the show's house band, as the show had strict rules about allowing any outside musicians like myself perform. It proved to be another long and busy day as most of it was spent rehearsing for the evening performance with crew and other performers kept busy throughout the day. In between rehearsals we managed to take a walk to St Kilda pier, taking in the breath-taking views.

The next morning it was an early start again as I escorted Steve back to the airport to board his flight back to England. We shared an early breakfast in the hotel and spent some time talking about the past week and plans for the future. I would be heading to Europe later that year in September to embark on my first European tour and we planned to catch up again in London. Once breakfast was over, and Steve had checked out we made our way to Melbourne airport where Steve boarded his late morning flight home.

8 - GUITAR HEROES

I n the aftermath of the birth of rock 'n' roll in the 1950s, instrumental guitar-driven music became part of the cultural lexicon. Early guitar pioneers such as Duane Eddy and Link Wray, whose fuzz-laden 1958 hit 'Rumble' was slapped with a ban on American radio, became the first guitar heroes, which later saw instrumental combos such as The Ventures in the United States and the hugely influential The Shadows in the UK, steer instrumental rock through its halcyon days of popularity over the next few years. The early 1960s surf music craze further solidified the genre, before the British Invasion took over, and instrumental music faded into the background only to re-emerge in the Progressive Rock period of the early 70s.

In the 1980s a renewed interest in the genre resurfaced, in the hands of more flamboyant six-string practitioners such as Americans Joe Satriani and Steve Vai. Though the style had moved on from the more simple approach of the genre's early years, it had now morphed into a more virtuoso style where technical skill was the primary driving force that directed the visceral and melodic aspects of the music.

For instrumental guitar legend Joe Satriani – better known as Satch - the genre has been his passport to a thirty plus year career in music. In 1987 Satriani released his second studio outing, *Surfing With The Alien,* which brought him commercial success and established him as a solo artist in his own right. The album mixed elements from rock to jazz to heavy metal into a nicely concise framework that, though heavy on the shred factor, was still strong on melody. The commercial success and critical acclaim for the album led to the resurgence of the instrumental genre, and a number of tracks from the album made it into the mainstream charts.

Satriani had previously been an in-demand guitar tutor, many of his former students went on to become influential guitarists in their own right such as Kirk Hammett from Metallica and Steve Vai, who followed in his former tutor's footsteps with a similar styled album with 1990's *Passion And Warfare*.

Around the time of *Surfing With The Aliens*, Satriani had been touring the world as guitarist as part of Mick Jagger's solo back-up band. With relations between himself and fellow Rolling Stone Keith Richards fractured, Jagger had invited Satriani to join him on tour which helped raise Joe's profile substantially, and turned the fortunes around for his solo album. After the Jagger tour Satriani moved forward in a solo capacity and onto a cycle of recording albums and touring in support of them. Over the years he continued to build a solid back catalogue while continuing to push the sonic envelope of what was possible within the boundaries of the guitar. Life on the road became Satriani's second home. The Jagger tour taught Satriani a lot about the sacrifices required on the often lengthy stints on the road. For Satriani, first and foremost, it requires a disciplined mental approach. Once he is onstage, his mind will shift into a different state. His guitar tech is one of the most important people around him, playing an integral role in helping the guitarist to maintain and able to perform his nightly sets faultlessly.

"I kind of lose track of what's going on when I'm on stage" he told me. "I get so deep into the music that once

From Top: Interviewing Steve Vai in 2004 at the Palace in St Kilda; Steve signing posters in December 2006 after his Regent Theatre gig and interviewing Joe Satriani in Melbourne in 2005.

it's over, it takes me quite a long time to regain my mental capacities."

By the time I first met Satriani in early 2005, his latest tour had clocked up over 150,000 miles and had already taken in shows in 26 countries in support of his latest album *Is There Love in Space?* his tenth studio offering. For an artist of his calibre his choice of set list, consisting of as many as thirty songs per night, required careful consideration. At times his shows would stretch out to three hours.

For a solo artist a backing band is the most important cog in the wheel. If the band are tight, and locked into a groove, the chemistry between the musicians will form a bond allowing Satriani the freedom to do what he does so well. For the 2005 tour Satriani tapped drummer Jeff Campitelli - who he had known since 1979 - and bassist Matt Bissonette as his primary backing band. The touring line-up was rounded off by the addition of Galen Henson on rhythm guitar, who also served as tour manager.

I met up with Satriani at his hotel in Melbourne, alongside his long-time manager Mick Brigden. Brigden had quite an illustrious back story himself, having been former road-manager for Humble Pie, Mountain and Peter Frampton. He shared some stories with us about his time spent being a road manager. After introductions were made, the day's schedule was given a final look over, I jumped into the Tarago van with them and we were escorted to The Forum where Joe would be performing later that evening. The Forum has played host to numerous international acts over the years having first opened in 1929 as a cinema and eventually in the 1980s it morphed into a live concert venue with standing capacity for approximately 2,000. Upon arrival we made our way down to the dressing room, a spacious area surrounded by concrete walls - the perfect place to prepare, as the walls blocked out all outside noise. A large table was set up with sandwiches, various fruits and salads and a selection of beers, bottled water and wine.

Moments later Satriani made his way back to the stage to begin sound check. I met his guitar tech Mike who showed me around and explained the show's format. He explained that with recent shows nearing the three hour mark per evening, it was important to showcase a set list that was strong and far reaching to encapsulate Satriani's career. With an extensive back catalogue, the song choices were paramount along with Joe's pre-show ritual. "He likes to warm up for about 30 minutes before a show doing simple exercises" he told me, "That is so he could get used to the structures and all the bending stuff that he'll be needing to play later in the show". While talking to me Mike was constantly kept running to and fro, making sure everything was working right and any technical hitches that may cause an issue later in the show were anticipated and rectified.

Satriani ran though a couple numbers from the coming evening's set list, but it wasn't long before it morphed into an all-out jam session with the band. Joe later explained that during these types of 'jams' musical ideas would come to him, which he would continue working on as the tour went forward, and which he would eventually turn into a new song or two. A lot of initial song ideas tended to come on the road. Finally, as Satriani headed off to the privacy of his dressing room to prepare for show time with guitar in hand, he sat down and for the next thirty minutes as part of his pre-show ritual performed simple warm up finger exercises. I left him to it as he closed the door. I made my way to the side of the stage and waited until show time.

When Joe finally hit the stage, the audience let out a

loud roar which echoed across the Forum's walls. Kicking proceedings off with opener 'Up In The Sky' (from his 1998 album, *Crystal Planet*), and pulling out all stops, he delivered a magnificent and dazzling three-hour set comprising older numbers and newer ones off his latest album.

After the show he made his way back to his dressing room, where he quickly closed the door behind him so he could regain his composure following the adrenaline rush having expending all his energy on his performance. After about thirty minutes Joe opened the door and the preparations began for his departure back to the hotel. At this point, I thanked him for his time and for allowing me to join him on tour. I would next spend three days with him when he was in town again in December 2006 as part of the G3 tour. G3 is a touring show that was first put together by Satriani and Steve Vai. The first show, which featured the line-up of Joe Satriani, Eric Johnson and Steve Vai, took place in 1996. The *modus operandi* of the show was to bring together three of the finest guitarists of the moment onto the same stage. The shows are usually divided into four sections. Each player will perform their own set of material then afterwards all three come together for the finale which is usually a huge jam session. The jam tends to feature a selection of well-known rock and blues numbers. The G3 festival made its way to Australia for the first time that December where they played to sold-out shows across the country.

Included on the Australian tour itinerary were two shows at the Regent Theatre in Melbourne, a historic former picture palace that was originally built in 1929, with ornately palatial styled architecture it was the perfect setting for the six-string festival.

Satriani invited me to spend three days with him and the rest of the G3 guitarists while they were in town. The brief was to observe everything from behind the scenes as a fly on the wall, which made for a fascinating and eye-opening experience. A tremendous amount of planning and logistics is involved in bringing such a huge festival together and it is just as demanding for the performers. I asked Joe how performing a G3 show compared to performing his own headlining show, "Well our own shows are incredibly demanding just from my left arm [laughs] because I'm playing all those melodies and solos that require some much squeezing and bending. It is a very different kind of technique than if you were just playing in a band and playing rhythm most of the time and then doing a couple of solo breaks. And the more blues phrasing I work into it, the harder it is to keep that going for say a three-hour show. It's very demanding. Like I play at the top of the song, I play the melody. I play the solo you know, song after song after song. It's very intense but also very satisfying. At the end of the show, I always feel like I've played every possible thing I can play that evening. I feel very artistically drained but happy. But it does take a lot of work."

The G3 were all staying at the upmarket Hilton Hotel down the road from the venue and had flown into Melbourne very early that Saturday morning from their Sydney show the previous night. I was originally scheduled to meet up with all three guitarists (Satriani, Vai and John Petrucci) on the Saturday, the day of the first Melbourne show, at 2.00pm for their sound check. Somehow, I ended up waiting a good four and half hours before I finally got in! I was told sound check was running late and that none of the three of them were present. So, I waited and waited.

But hey, this is rock 'n' roll where most of the time nothing runs to schedule anyway.

Eventually Mick Brigden surfaced and after a warm welcome kindly escorted me backstage. First stop was the production office where I was given my AAA pass which allowed me to roam free backstage. My first port of call was to head for the stage where Petrucci was in the midst of sound checking his set with Mike Portnoy on drums and Dave La Rue on bass.

Both Petrucci and Portnoy were founding members of their main 'day job' band, Dream Theatre, a progressive metal outfit. Petrucci had released his first solo outing, *Suspended Animation*, a year earlier. They blasted through a song while crew and tech guys scrambled about with their gear. I hung around sound check for awhile afterwards, observing the many guitars and walls of amplifiers set up on stage. I also recognized familiar faces in Satriani's crew from my time with Joe in early 2005 when he was last in Melbourne.

Wandering through the corridors of the venue I spotted bassist extraordinaire Billy Sheehan who was walking to his dressing room. He was kitted out in his stage gear which included shiny black vinyl pants and spaceman-like high-heel boots, he looked younger than 53. Sheehan's clean living ways were certainly paying him dividends. He later told me that aside from abstaining from drink, drugs and cigarettes, he had avoided prescription or over the counter drugs such as aspirin, which he said he had last taken back in 1972!

Next I ran into Steve Vai who I had first interviewed on the phone in 2002 and again in 2004. It was great to finally meet him in person and spend time with him backstage on the day of his show in Melbourne in July 2004 on his solo tour. On that tour, he performed at The Palace and I spent the afternoon with him and the most memorable thing about my interviews was his interest and passion for beekeeping! Vai, looking in good shape, remembered me from our meeting. His friendship with Sheehan went back decades and both had played together in David Lee Roth's band in the late 1980s. In another dressing room Sheehan sat on a couch practicing with his bass in hand and wearing ear headphones while Tony McAlpine, who had forged a successful solo career as an instrumentalist, sat in a corner running through some shredding licks on the guitar.

Further up the hallway I passed the dressing room of Portnoy and Petrucci. Petrucci was in the midst of getting changed into his stage clothes, so I quickly introduced myself and wished him all the best for the show. Once he had changed, he sat practicing his guitar along with a metronome while Portnoy readied himself for the show and changed into his stage clothes too. At this point Joe Satriani was nowhere to be found, though he would turn up later.

As show time loomed Petrucci, La Rue and Portnoy assembled in the hallway and high-fived each other with enthusiasm before making their way to the stage. Doors were due to open at 7pm but because things were running slightly late, the show didn't begin until 7.40pm when Petrucci hit the stage. With the room only half full but slowly filling, he performed a blistering and well received set. Due to a personal emergency matter I had to attend to, I had to quickly depart for home, just as Petrucci was playing the final bars of his last song, so I missed the rest of the show.

I returned the next day – Sunday - for the second and final show of their Melbourne G3 stint and again with

AAA pass in hand, spent considerable time conversing with all backstage, in dressing rooms and later, side of stage as well, to watch the whole remarkable four-hour set.

Earlier that day all three guitarists had performed at a nearby music store in the city. Backstage there were five rooms allocated to the G3 artists: Vai had two, Satch had one which was much larger than the others and Petrucci had two. A catering area was set up down the other end of the corridor right next to the stage door area where hot meals and desserts were on offer. In the dressing rooms each was equipped with copious amounts of bottled water, fruit and sandwiches.

Petrucci, Portnoy and LaRue hit the stage to perform their set to a rapturous welcome. It was a full house again. Petrucci and co laid the crowd to waste, the onstage interaction of each musician was superb which showed by much smiling between each and satisfaction with their performance. Vai's guitar tech Thomas came and collected a couple of Ibanez guitars from his dressing room. The crowd roared and rose from their seats as the band ended their set. Portnoy took to the mic and said, 'Melbourne, Australia, John Petrucci'. Cue more loud applause. All three then made their way to the side of the stage and to their dressing rooms.

Once Petrucci and co. finished their set, the crew quickly hit the stage to do an equipment change over for the next set as they gathered in their dressing rooms and took stock of their great show. Vai was all dressed up and ready to go and called his band (McAlpine – guitar/keyboards, Sheehan – bass, Dave Weiner – rhythm guitar, Jeremy Colson – drums) into his room for a last minute group gathering before hitting the stage to rapturous applause as Billy chatted with me about live photography while waiting to go on. He told me the best photos were those that had the artist and the crowd in front. He held a beer in one hand whilst his left hand ran through some bass exercises. He then headed on stage.

Backstage Satriani had arrived in his dressing room and was warming up. I took some candid shots of this process. Petrucci was in there too, signing the same posters that Vai had earlier. Petrucci looked refreshed after his show. Satch readied himself by strumming on a guitar in his room while drummer Jeff Campitelli performed some leg and arm stretching exercises to warm up. Satriani then made his way to the side of stage to watch Vai's performance before returning to his dressing room for one last time. Vai played a wailing lick which suddenly became a call and response with the audience. The power of his playing was incredible. Vai finished his set with 'For the Love Of God', his body becoming one with the guitar, even taking his tongue onto the guitar and creating a squealing effect that was otherworldly. Vai and band returned to their dressing room drenched in sweat and with smiles on their faces after an explosive set. Vai's dressing room then closed again and the backstage area became eerily quiet.

The crew again quickly did another change over to prepare for Satriani's set. It was very hectic onstage, guys were rushing to and fro. I was chatting to some lighting guys who told me some war stories as Satriani and his band (LaRue - bass, Galen Henson – rhythm guitar, Jeff Campitelli – drums) psyched themselves up.

The production manager came to collect Satriani and his band and escorted them on stage. All let out a "good on you mate" chant before departing the room and for the stage. Petrucci came to the side stage area to grab his guitar and walked back to his room. Vai walked to the side of the stage too and grabbed his Ibanez. Sheehan walked down the corridor of the backstage area, glass of wine in one hand and handed me some of his bass picks. Vai walked to his room with guitar in hand. He asked me if I got a copy of his set list yet, I tell him no, he replies, "I'll tell you as it was a short one, you have a pen and paper?" and proceeded to tell me his set.

I headed for the other side of the stage where Vai's guitar tech has setup shop. He handed me a copy of his set list too and one of Vai's picks. Vai came to side of stage where his tech was and prepared to join Satriani for the jam section of the show. He put on a cowboy hat and stood ready for his cue. Vai walked onstage to join Satriani playing some licks. Soon after Petrucci also joined them onstage from the other side of the stage and all broke out into a jam of Hendrix's 'Voodoo Chile'. The show finishes just thirty minutes short of midnight with an explosive rendition of Neil Young's 'Rockin' In The Free World'. For guitarists everywhere, G3 proved to be a brilliant and exhilarating six-string extravaganza.

On Monday afternoon I headed back into town to their hotel for lengthy interviews with each guitarist. As I walked into the plush surrounds of The Hilton, I came across Sheehan who was frantically pacing the foyer. Dave La Rue walked in from outside with a cup of coffee in hand and headed straight to his hotel room upstairs. Vai then strolled in casually from outside too and headed for his room.

I walked into a quieter area of the dining area to wait for Satriani who would be my first interviewee for the day. A short time later he surfaced, we sat in the corner of the dining area and I conducted the interview. After my interview with Satriani was done, Vai was next in line.

This was followed by my final interviewee for the day, John Petrucci. Interestingly, Petrucci had just come back from an intense work-out at the gym. He told me that it was something he enjoyed doing while on tour. He also added that he actually walked the long distance to the gym but then afterwards grabbed a cab back to the hotel so he wouldn't be late for his interview.

The whole G3 camp remained in Melbourne for another day to take in the sights before heading off to their next show at Thebarton Theatre in Adelaide on the Wednesday. After about two solid hours of interviews, my three day adventure with G3 was finally coming to an end, and we said our goodbyes. I thanked one and all for the hospitality they'd shown me and for the wonderful opportunity given to me for the past three days. It had been a truly memorable experience and one I still cherish today.

9 - PROG-ROCK PROPHETS

English Prog-rockers YES are one of the true dinosaurs of rock. First formed in 1968, their cocktail of virtuoso musicianship laced with tapestries of sonic colours and melody pushed progressive rock into a wider mainstream audience. Their sometimes wild and often comedic adventures on the road and the often ludicrous spoils of success brought the band much fame, and much myth making, with many of the 'myths' proven to be fact rather than fiction. One particular incident concerned YES keyboard wizard Rick Wakeman and his predisposition for eating curries on stage and has become the stuff of legend.

YES first toured Australia in March 1973 as part of their *Close To The Edge* tour, with the band riding high at the time and forging their place in music history. It would take another thirty years before the band returned to Australia in September 2003 as part of their 35th Anniversary world tour that included three Australian dates in Melbourne, Sydney and Perth. They had been scheduled to tour earlier that year but had to reschedule all their dates due to singer Jon Anderson having suffered a serious spinal injury. It was on this tour that I got to meet and interview the band for the first time and see their Melbourne show.

The tour saw the classic line-up together again, the same line-up that had toured back in 1973; Jon Anderson on vocals, Steve Howe on guitar, Chris Squire on bass, Alan White on drums and Rick Wakeman – who over the thirty years had already left and returned numerous times to the band but had again re-joined in 2002 - on keyboards. He would depart the band for good in 2004 and his son Oliver replaced him in 2008.

With his trademark long flowing blond hair, flowing cape and encircled by rows of keyboards, Rick defined the excesses of 1970s rock 'n' roll and has claimed that his exploits provided the inspiration for the famed 1984 mockumentary, *This Is Spinal Tap*. At one point Rick had amassed a collection of Rolls-Royces. He also had an illustrious career on the sidelines as a session player for numerous classics. That's him playing the piano on Cat Steven's evergreen hit, 'Morning Has Broken', and him playing the Mellotron on David Bowie's 'Changes' among others. He is also a television personality, and a regular on the British TV series *Grumpy Old Men* where he moans about 21st century life.

My first point of call on a day of interviews was to make my way to the 31st floor of the upmarket Grand Hyatt Hotel. It's the perfect locale for media interviews, with the floor imbued with a serene and ambient quality back dropped by spectacular views of the Melbourne skyline. Upon arrival two other media personnel were already there chatting with the record label publicist as they waited for the band to arrive.

First to arrive and enter the room was drummer Alan White who, quickly greeting everyone, is introduced to his interviewer from a local drum magazine. White is and remains to this day one of the band's longest serving members. Next up were Jon Anderson – who would eventually exit the band in 2008 due to health reasons – and Rick Wakeman. Rick quickly lightens the mood, cracking some jokes as he is introduced to all present, causing all present in the room to burst out in hearty laughter. As the laughter dies down, he takes a seat in front of a make shift

TV set, to begin an interview with an online website.

Steve Howe is running late so I just wait around. He finally arrives about twenty minutes later. We are introduced and he takes his seat opposite me, near one of the windows and tells me that they've only just arrived in town earlier that morning from Tokyo. He looks very tired and dishevelled but he remains pleasant and enthusiastic during the interview. I notice he looks older than he is and his teeth are all rotten, hair thinning and stringy and overly grey. While the others in the band looked in better shape all around, as a result Steve looks like the odd one out. Wearing light coloured and very casual clothing, with a throwback 1980s-style beige and brown slip-on shoes, he seems more like a grandfather than a rock star. He is also the first artist who quietly requests that no photo is to be taken of him in this state as he admits to me, 'I don't look too good today'. He adds that he will be happy to oblige me with a photo the next day after the show after he has rested and is more comfortable.

He gave me forty-five minutes of his time, and happily talked to me about YES, Asia, his guitar playing and various other musical topics of interest. Being a guitarist myself, I was particularly interested in his influences. He affirmed that his all-time favourite guitarist was American finger picking country guitarist Chet Atkins. He also mentioned to me that one of the most influential tracks on his playing was 'Classical Gas', an instrumental guitar piece by American guitarist Mason Williams that came out in 1968. "When 'Classical Gas' came out I used to say 'that was me' because that was exactly what I was trying to do" Howe told me before adding, "I sat down and learned it because to me, that could have been written by me, if only I had written it. It was exactly the kind of guitar music I loved so much", which summed up Howe precisely to the type of guitarist he himself had become and was respected for. He also shared with me a story that involved 'Classical Gas' and the legendary British guitarist Eric Clapton. "I actually played that song for him one time" he revealed. "It was back in the early '70's when we shared a hotel together somewhere. He asked me if I could play 'Classical Gas' and, trying to impress him, said 'Yes'. So, I sat there and played it for him. Once I finished, Eric turned to me and said 'that's great!'

By the time my interview with Howe was up, the rest of the band had departed, except for the band's record label publicist and one other journalist who was hanging around listening in to our interview. With everyone now gone, the atmosphere in the room was so quiet you could hear a pin drop. After the interview we took the elevator down to the floor where Steve was staying. The elevator gets half way down before it stops and Steve bid us goodbye and left. As he leaves, he turns around and asks us if we could recommend a good vegetarian restaurant as he is in need of some food. We direct him to a nearby restaurant a short walk from the hotel.

The label publicist confirms that I have an interview with Rick Wakeman the following day he also confirms that I will be able to meet him backstage after the show the next evening. One noticeable absence during the whole time I was in the hotel was bassist Chris Squire, who was nowhere to seen during the entire time I was there and the rest of the day. As I made way down the city streets, I spotted Alan White walking down the street and going into a pub for some beers. Visiting the pub seems to be a rite of passage with English bands. In all my meetings and interviews with British bands over the years, the thing I noticed that was a constant was their passion for finding the nearest pub and enjoying a beer. Many bands have told me that they tend to pick studios that are located near pubs so that once the work is done, they can quickly pop in and drink the rest of the day (or night) away. The same *modus operandi* seems to be the case while on tour!

Later that evening my wife and I made our way to Vodafone Arena to watch YES perform. From our vantage point we watched the show slowly deteriorate into a train wreck as it was plagued by non-stop technical problems both on and off stage. The poor attendance of around 4,000, well below the 10,000 capacity, must have put more stress on the band. Support for the show that night was provided by Australian prog-rock outfit Sebastian Hardie, a band that had been around since the later part of the 1960s, had broken up and then reformed again, only to split up and then reform once again specifically for their support slot with YES. Led by guitarist Mario Millo, the band started the evening stridently, but things soon took a turn that marred the rest of the evening.

The troubles began when the support band suffered the wrath of YES's crew, when running a few minutes over their allocated 30 minutes, they literally had the power plug pulled from them midway through a song by Steve Howe's guitar technician. There was a sudden dead silence. Surprised by what happened and the crew members unprofessionalism, Millo apologised to the audience, and stated that their set only had minutes left to go. People started booing and displayed their displeasure at what had just occurred. Tempers between crew members began to flare and arguments broke out, all in front of the prying eyes of the stunned audience.

Then once YES hit the stage things continued to go

downhill. Numerous times during the show extraneous feedback continuously interfered during the band's set. Steve Howe suffered the brunt of the technical issues. Maybe it was Karma for what had ensued earlier, or maybe just co-incidence but it clearly started when Howe was about to perform the song 'And You And I'. An incessant discordant hissing and crackling sound plagued his acoustic guitar. Becoming annoyed with it, he quickly picked up an electric guitar, which unbeknown to him had not had been tuned, which again led him to again abandon the song, and restart again, once the guitar was tuned. Howe tried soldiering on while his guitar tech frantically trying to rectify the issue.

Later, as Anderson began to sing, the extraneous feedback had deteriorated so badly that he stopped and called a halt to the song. Trying to save face he tried to make light of the situation by stating, "This happens every night, its part of the show...We've got to practice more, I just know it, we want to get it right". He then surprised everyone, including the band itself, by announcing that Rick would provide some comedic relief while the crew tried to find a solution to the noise issue. Rick, surprised by Anderson's request, left his keyboards and began making his way to the front of the stage, and called out, "Tell me you're ready, Steve! You ready?" To which Howe replied, "Yes". Relieved, Rick told the audience, "I'll have to tell it another time then. What a shame!" and returned to his keyboards. But as the band kicked into the song, the timing was all over the place, and they were all playing in the wrong key. Anderson again stopped proceedings and requested a restart telling the audience, "It didn't sound in key". The audience looked both amused and confused.

The stop-start-stop-start process affected the show's

flow and momentum and Howe in particular seemed to bear the brunt of it for the rest of the night's performance and with their on-stage banter to the audience kept to a minimum, it didn't help their cause. Again, when it came for his solo spot during 'To Be Over' the sound issues from earlier on resurfaced. Visually frustrated he eventually abandoned the song, and just played his classically inspired instrumental 'Clap' on electric instead. Once the show was over, the band left the stage, only to return minutes later for an encore, that included a highly energized and abridged version of 'Roundabout' and finally got everyone up and dancing, capping off a surprisingly unusual ending to a prog rock show.

Backstage at a YES concert is quite strange; there were a few hangers on, some looking as if they had not moved on from their hippie days, who made their presence known to all the band members. Chris Squire walked around totally inebriated while Steve Howe seemed lost as he walked around, came into the room where we were, took one look, turned around and left to go back to his hotel room. Rick held court and provided much comedic relief for all and helped lighten the mood, his genuinely friendly nature tinged with a sense of humour and a warm-hearted spirit, kept us entertained and enthralled. His down to earth attitude was refreshing. In that backstage room Rick became the centre of attention. He later apologized for not being able to do the planned interview earlier in the day, but asked me to return the next.

The next morning, I met Rick in the lobby of his hotel and he explained the previous day's drama and said the band were not happy with the crew member who pulled the plug on the support band but also explained that they needed to fit their set within the constraints of the venue's curfew rules. Because Rick was due to fly out of Melbourne later that morning, we quickly got to the task at hand as time was limited. He was happy to answer any of my questions regardless of subject matter and was very forthcoming, open and honest. During the entire interview Rick punctuated our conversation with one-liners that turned the interview into an enjoyable, uplifting experience. It was as if two mates were conversing in the confines of a pub over some beers. There was no pretence whatsoever on Rick's behalf. Both my initial meeting the night before and that day left a lasting impression on me.

One of the privileges inherent in my line of work as a music journalist is the behind the scenes access I am granted. With it comes an opportunity to view what lies behind the public persona of a performer and musician, which often can often be at odds with their onstage persona. An Access All Areas pass is a passport to unlocking the door into the private world of the artist, and seeing them in their unedited form free of press agents and PR gurus. From my experience I've found many tend to perpetuate an image that is in stark contrast to their private selves, a fact that is par for the course in the music industry but when it comes to someone like Rick Wakeman no such distinction exists.

After that YES tour in 2003, Wakeman made a welcome return to Australia two years later where I had the privilege of spending the weekend with the man while he was on his solo tour, which he had stated at the time, was going to be his last ever Down Under. There were two dates in late August at Hamer Hall and another two in Sydney. Special guest with Wakeman on the tour was a man named Ashley Holt whose background included being one of two singers (the other being Ian Gillan) shortlisted for the vocal spot in legendary rock band Deep Purple in the band's original incarnation. Wakeman's relationship with Holt went as far back as 1965 when Rick, as a sixteen year-old, auditioned for Holt's band.

Holt had toured Australia with Wakeman back in 1975 on the latter's *Journey To The Centre Of The Earth* tour. Again I found Wakeman to be exactly as he was upon our first meeting two years earlier. As on the previous occasion, his inviting and open nature was contagious both onstage and off. I spent the weekend with him and Holt during rehearsals, sound check and then later for dinner and the show.

Resplendent in a pink coat that featured large musical notes all over it, Wakeman looked every bit the eccentric keyboard wizard. The Saturday night show that he performed using a Steinway Grand Piano and various other keyboards was basically a greatest hits set that covered a selection of tracks that were largely focused on his earlier solo outings from such albums as *The Six Wives of Henry VIII* (1973), *Journey to the Centre of the Earth* (1974), *The Myths and Legends of King Arthur and the Knights of the Round Table* (1975) as well as a sprinkling of other tracks from the latter part of his illustrious career and, as an added crowd pleaser, a couple of Beatles covers thrown in for good measure. The songs were interspersed with Wakeman retelling various comedic anecdotes. To me his show bore a slight resemblance to the halcyon years of the late great Victor Borge and his one-man shows that featured a mix of comedy and piano music. At one point Wakeman threw on a pre-recorded DVD featuring orchestra and choir to back his performance of 'The Dance of a Thousand Lights', a track off his rather recent *Return To The Centre Of The Earth* album from 1999 which, from the reaction it received from the seated audience, proved to be a highlight.

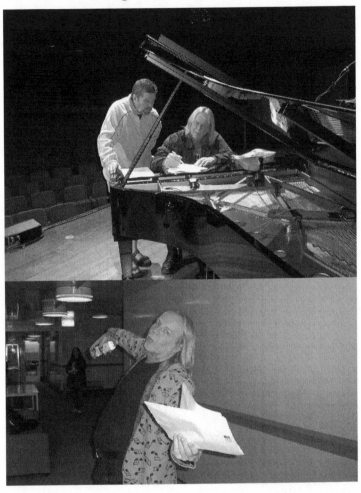

Ashley Holt and Rick Wakeman pre-show rehearsal at Hamer Hall, 2005; Rick hamming it up backstage at the same venue.

And Wakeman definitely knew how to keep the audience entertained while sharing his stories. The pick of the crop was the true, but hilarious and Spinal Tap-ish tale of his drunken mid-70s Seattle stop-over at the Paramount Theatre. Another was his recollection of the time his mother and ten geriatric friends of hers visited Wakeman at one of his sold-out London shows in the early 1980s. And another was about his late friend Marc Bolan, when Bolan asked Rick to play a simple piano glissando [where the fingers swipe across the keys in one motion] on 'Get It On'. To which Rick replied, 'You could have done that yourself,' where upon Bolan responded 'Well, you want your rent money don't you?' These stories and others had the audience in stitches. The man was a wonderful story teller, hugely funny, sincere and most of all had his feet firmly planted on the ground. Sunday's show was similar to the previous night's though with a slightly rearranged set list and a few differing anecdotes.

One particular anecdote he shared recalled a show YES had performed at the Manchester Free Trade Hall in the early Seventies. The caped wonder, feeling bored and a little hungry had instructed one of the crew to put in a take away order for some Vindaloo curry. When the crew member arrived backstage later with Wakeman's food order, the whole band were midway through a song. The crew member proceeded to hand over tin foiled containers of curry to Wakeman who then placed them on top of his keyboards. Once the portion of the song began where Wakeman had not much to do playing wise, and away from the glare of the stage lights, with the food itself hidden from the audience's view by the numerous rows of keyboards, he began tucking into his curry while the show continued on. The curry's strong aroma eventually penetrated the stage air, so much so that vocalist Jon Anderson, curious to find out where the smell was coming from, followed its trail towards Wakeman. Anderson took one look at his fellow band member, threw him a look of utter disbelief, shrugged his shoulders, turned around and returned centre stage, continuing his singing as if nothing had happened.

He also recounted another incident where a female fan turned up at a show asking Wakeman if he could sign her G-string? Only problem was, she wanted him to sign it while she was wearing it!

At the end of the Sunday performance, a select group of VIP ticket holders were treated to a private audience with Wakeman and Holt that offered up a Q & A session followed by signings and photos. Afterwards greetings and well wishes were exchanged as preparations were made for Wakeman and his entourage to depart Melbourne for Sydney the next day. At that point I bid him farewell and thanked him for his time and hospitality. God knows we need more people like Wakeman in the world at present to keep reminding all of us that we really shouldn't take ourselves too seriously. His humour was certainly contagious, his charm irresistible and his keyboard wizardry, truly magical. In June 2021 Wakeman became the proud recipient of a CBE (Commander of the Order of the British Empire) for his services to music and broadcasting.

10 - METAL GODS

Heavy metal is one genre of music that is more than just about the music itself. Encompassing fashion, culture and an inclusive community spirit, it is also a unique way of life. Having spent many years interviewing metal acts and witnessing first hand the ethos and spirit of brotherhood that exists within the metal community, I have learned that it is also one of the most misunderstood genres to the run of the mill music fan. One of the most striking features of metal bands is how much of the image and music is worlds apart from the person making it. There is always a huge disconnect between a band's 'evil' image and the lyrical content of the music. Metal musicians understand that much of their public persona and performances is purely musical theatre and so there is a distinction between fantasy and reality.

You'd be surprised at the contrasts in character and personality of what one sees on the stage or television or reads about in the tabloid press, to what they're like in person in the privacy of their own space away from the stage. A classic example of the huge misunderstanding of the genre are metal titans Black Sabbath, a band that came out of the industrial city of Birmingham and are credited as being godfathers of metal, and who have made a career out of its occult subject matter. The band's bassist and lyricist Geezer Butler is largely credited with the occultist lyrical content but he was brought up as a strict Christian and credits his religious upbringing with his interest in the dark side.

Yet since their inception Sabbath have been misunderstood by religious institutions and the public at large. At the opposite end of the spectrum, they even had some fans conducting black magic rituals in the hallways of hotels they were staying in at the time. As Geezer told me in 2006, "as usual we got the wrong end of it. By the time Sabbath was going, the first song 'Black Sabbath' was actually a warning against being involved in the occult, but people didn't really listen to the lyrics, They just heard the name and assumed we were all Satanists".

American writer William Burroughs is widely credited with coining the actual phrase 'heavy metal' in his 1961 novel *The Soft Machine*, where he describes one of the book's characters as 'the Heavy Metal Kid' though the term can actually be traced back to the 19th century when heavy metal poisoning was a common medical term. It later appeared for the first time in a song on Steppenwolf's 1968 motorcycle rock anthem 'Born To Be Wild'. I've had some fascinating insights into a lot of the metal artists' character and psyche, and have been pleasantly surprised many times to see that behind the 'stage mask' lie decent, courteous, well-mannered and well-behaved human beings. One thing that remains a constant is their passion for their lifestyle and music, their loyalty to their fans and community and their unwavering dedication to their art.

I've been fortunate enough to not only interview many metal bands but to have spent time with them backstage and on the road. I interviewed American metal act Disturbed on numerous occasions during the 2000s. I first interviewed and met the band during their first ever Australian tour in February, 2003. There was a lot of hype surrounding the band at the time, especially after the Prince of Darkness himself, Ozzy Osbourne, said of the band, "I have seen the future of metal". Disturbed had just released their second album *Believe* (2002) a few months earlier, and a lot was riding on the band after the huge success they had garnered in the aftermath of their debut release *The Sickness* (2000). With only three shows in Australia spread over a space of a few days, their Australian record label Warner Music worked them hard and ensured every moment the band were not travelling or performing was taken up with promotional duties for the album.

They were holed up at the Grand Hyatt, a hotel of choice for many visiting international touring acts and celebrities in Melbourne. Once more my interviews with them would take place on the 31st floor against a backdrop of the Melbourne skyline. Once I arrived, I was quickly greeted by the band's publicist who introduced me to the band's chrome-domed vocalist David Draiman. With his double labret piercing, that bore a strong resemblance to a pair of talons hanging from his chin, he struck an imposing image. Add the fact he wore tight black leather pants, it certainly added mystique to his image of a Metal God. Draiman was about to sit down and have some dinner as the band had just arrived on a flight from Sydney a few hours earlier, where they had played their first ever Australian show the previous night. The band had been put to work the moment they set foot in Melbourne, so Draiman wanted to take a short break to have some food to refuel before continuing with his press obligations. While he went away and had dinner, I was offered a drink and asked to relax until he had eaten so that interviews could continue.

The band's guitarist (and keyboardist) Dan Donegan, also dressed in black leather pants, finally walked in after having just completed an interview so I was brought to him so we could be introduced and after his dinner, Draiman, Donegan and I were escorted into an adjoining room for the interview. Donegan left his sunglasses on for the entire interview, possibly to cover the red eyes caused by the late night and early flight. Although Draiman took charge of the interview and was very dominant throughout, he was respectful of Donegan and shared his interview time equally. At the end I thanked them for their time and wish them luck for the show later that evening, and mention that I'd be seeing them there. As I was escorted back to the elevator the publicist tells me the boys have one more interview to do before heading to the sound check.

I arrived at 9pm that evening to catch Disturbed's show at the Hi-fi Bar & Ballroom. An underground venue hidden away down a flight of stairs off Swanston Street, one of the city's busiest thoroughfares, a venue of choice for many visiting metal bands. Up and coming new Australian industrial metal outfit Jerk were playing support, and were finishing their set as I arrived. The 800+ capacity room was a sell-out and ticketless fans were lining up outside the venue on the off chance of getting in but were politely asked to leave. The place was packed to the rafters as a thirty minute interval ensued before Disturbed hit the stage to rapturous applause. The members of Jerk were already in right in front of the stage where they banged their heads away throughout the band's set. With special access authorized by the label, I was allocated one of the best viewing spots, upstairs in the glass window room that was usually reserved for VIP and special guests.

Back dropped by the *Believe* album cover logo, which hid a wall of amplifiers, the band played a solid hour long set that included a ball busting cover of the Tears For Fears classic 'Shout'. With cries of, 'more, more' getting louder and louder, they returned to the stage and performed 'Prayer' and 'Stupify' as an encore before the show ended at around 11:00pm.

Three years later, I was dispatched to interview the band again, this time they were in town as part of a world tour supporting nu-metallers Korn on their *See You on the Other Side* World Tour. American metalcore outfit Hatebreed were also on the same bill. Disturbed were also doing promotional duties for their recently released third album *Ten Thousand Fists*. The show later that evening in Melbourne would be their final show of the Australian leg of the tour before Disturbed get off the tour, and headed back home to Chicago the very next day.

This time the interview occurred on a Saturday afternoon at The Langham Hotel, a plush, upper class place fitted with regal furnishings on a busy strip lined with shops and restaurants on Southbank Promenade along the Yarra River. The last time I was at The Langham was to interview rising Australian roots sensation John Butler in one of the suites on the upper floor when the hotel was known as Sheraton Towers.

As I entered the first level lounge area of the hotel David Draiman was sitting in the other part of the hotel's lounge area doing a television interview for a local youth broadcaster while the band's tour manager observed proceedings along with the band's record label publicist. I was re-introduced to Donegan again who recalled our previous interview a few years earlier. Dressed casually, he wore a tight sleeveless shirt, sneakers and a pair of cream coloured trousers, and had his hair in a ponytail. He answered my questions in-depth, always keeping eye contact, he spoke intelligently and with passion. I got told my interview was the last scheduled for the day, allowing them a few hours in the afternoon to relax and enjoy the delights of the city before their performance later that evening. Unfortunately I wasn't be able to make it to the show as I already had an engagement as a guest of Status Quo and Deep Purple who were also in town at the same time as part of a co-headlining tour billed as the *Double Trouble* Tour at the Palais Theatre in St. Kilda.

Hailing from Atlanta, Georgia, nu-metal quintet Sevendust had already released four studio albums; *Sevendust* (1997), *Home* (1999), *Animosity* (2001) and *Seasons* (2003) by the time they toured Australia for the very first time in March 2004. Australian fans of Sevendust had been disappointed by the cancellation of their first tour that was originally planned two years earlier in March 2002 when they would have undertaken a world tour with Creed. But a week before the tour was due to commence, Sevendust pulled out citing "undisclosed unforeseen circumstances."

"I love it here" Sevendust lead vocalist Lajon Witherspoon told me as we were sitting in the foyer of the stylish boutique Marque Hotel, nestled in vibrant beach side St. Kilda on a sunny weekday afternoon. In fact he loved it so much he told me he planned to start writing the band's next album there. "I've been enjoying the beach scenery here so it's providing much inspiration for me" . Heavily tattooed, tanned and dressed in a white tee-shirt and blue jeans, Witherspoon told me he had some early ideas already on the go. Eavesdropping on our conversation, and waiting in the wings was the band's Australian record label publicist, who suddenly interrupted our conversation to offer Witherspoon some advice; "Do not go into the waters of St. Kilda, instead go to Sydney's beaches as they're better!" she said, with an intensity in her voice that demanded your attention. As part of Sevendust's current Australian tour they were originally scheduled to perform in Adelaide later that evening but the show was cancelled due to low ticket sales and so the band had decided to make their way to Melbourne a day early so that they could have some free time to enjoy the sights and sounds. After Melbourne they would be heading back up to Sydney for the next show then onto Brisbane for the final show before they would make their way back to the States to embark on an upcoming U.S tour. Two more band members - guitarist Clint Lowery and bassist Vince Hornsby – walked into the foyer and upon seeing us, walked over and introduced themselves. After a bit of small talk, and feeling thirsty, both headed to the hotel's bar area to get themselves a drink.

The publicist informed Witherspoon that her boss would be meeting the band later that evening but later, during a pre-show rehearsal at the venue, she notified the band that neither she nor her boss would be able to make it to the gig or meet the band. Over the course of my career, there have been numerous times when I had noticed label representatives and publicists make their presence known at their artists' shows, to show support for those touring acts on their label roster. Howeveer with no publicist or record label representatives, the band - and their tour manager - were left to fend for themselves and make their way around the city to the shows. I was informed that apart from a phone interview with a local metal radio presenter I was the only journalist the band were doing an interview with while they were in the country. In the end it turned out that I had the honour of being the first Australian to actually witness the band doing sound check since Melbourne was the first show of the Australian tour.

We were escorted to a private lounge area in the hotel where the remaining band members joined us; Guitarist John Connolly and drummer Morgan Rose. What immediately struck me was that all the members of Sevendust had well-defined physiques, the result of their weight-lifting regime. Witherspoon, Rose and especially Hornsby were all very friendly and open with their replies to my questions. I sensed Connolly seemed a lot more reserved than the others while Lowery was very friendly and always cracking jokes. I felt he was the 'clown' of the band, someone who most likely pulled the pranks and brought some light hearted relief from the hard graft of touring. At one point Witherspoon enquired about "an Australian indigenous band" and I asked him to provide further details - it turned out he was interested in purchasing a CD of indigenous outfit Yothu Yindu who had a major hit with their song, 'Treaty' in the early part of the 1990s. 'Treaty' had the honour of being the first song by a predominantly Indigenous Australian band to achieve chart success in Australia. All made mention that they found Australian alcoholic drinks a lot stronger than their American counterparts. Witherspoon revealed that after having only drunk two beers the previous evening, he was already starting to feel the effects of the alcohol, while Rose laughed and stated that he had gotten wasted the night before having consumed eight beers, two cocktails and a few other beverages.

The band then received a message that their planned rehearsal scheduled for a 5:00pm start had been pushed back two hours. With their schedule now changed, and all feeling hungry, they decided to take a walk around St Kilda and find something to eat. I recommend some local eateries and took Lowery for a walk down the main street to show him what was on offer.

The purpose of the rehearsal that evening was the fact that they hadn't played together for about a month since they had finished their last US tour. The rehearsal was planned in order to get their chops back and to properly warm-up before the show. Finally, after walking a short distance around the corner to the venue, all arrived for rehearsal. The crew and roadies had set the stage up and there was gear strewn all around the place. The guitarists' respective racks were overloaded with guitars. Lowery's rack alone housed nine Paul Reed Smith guitars in different colours while Connolly's sported the same amount of Gibson Les Pauls and Epiphone Les Pauls with a sole Epiphone Explorer the odd guitar out. The backline featured a wall of Randall and Peavey amps with the drum kit set-up up on a platform about two feet above the main stage area. One of the crew had positioned and hidden himself behind the stage and was running a hard disc recorder so that he could record the show.

Once the band started to run through a song the mood lifted and the band felt in good spirits, Lowery suddenly launched into the opening riff to 'Unchained' by Van Halen. The rest of the band followed suit and ended up playing a blistering version of the song. Quickly after that they undertook a run through of 'Broken Down', the then current single taken off their *Seasons* album. With the time for opening doors getting closer by the minute, the band ended their rehearsal and headed backstage to change into their stage clothes.

With show time fast approaching the smell of weed permeated the air, and I noticed one of the crew positioned on the side of the stage smoking a huge cigar-sized joint.

The band finally hit the stage just before 11pm to rapturous applause. The mosh pit in front of the stage had already started going off, and for the next seventy minutes the band performed a blistering show. Kicking off proceedings with 'Black' (the band's 1997 debut single), it was quickly followed by 'Denial'. Witherspoon then asked the audience to sing along to 'Trust' if they knew the words, which they all did. He then dedicated 'Angel's Son' to his younger brother Reginald who had been fatally shot in Nashville a few months earlier. This was followed by 'Rumble Fish' during which Witherspoon called on the audience to "get up, get up, get up!" 'Enemy' began the encore before they grinded out the riff to Pantera's 'Walk' which segued into an extended version of Metallica's 'Master Of Puppets', which allowed the band to jam out for a while before they closed their set with 'Praise'.

As one of the most influential heavy metal bands of all, Metallica are also one of the most commercially successful of the genre and touring has been one of the constants for the band over the years, helping to build their much earned reputation as a huge draw card on the live touring circuit. The band first toured Australia back in 1989 and I first interviewed an (ex) member of Metallica back in 2002 when I spoke to former bass player Jason Newsted who had left the band a year earlier. That same year I also spoke to uber-producer Bob Rock during the middle of recording sessions for Metallica's *St. Anger* album which would see release in June 2003. My chat with Rock turned into an in-the-studio world exclusive news article that was published in *Guitar World* magazine in late 2002.

A month before official release of the album, in May

2003, Metallica's record label held a listening party at Chapel Off Chapel a former church building that had been converted into a theatre venue in the upscale inner suburb of Prahran. With interest in the new Metallica album high, being one of the invite-only media personnel, we all lined up outside the venue, eagerly waiting to be part of a select group who would be the first to listen to it outside of Europe. Security was tight and heavily adhered to, all our belongings such as phones were confiscated on entry and metal detectors were used on everybody.

Inside the room all the lights were dimmed, creating the perfect mood for listening while Metallica music blared out through the in-house PA. Food and alcoholic drinks were in plentiful supply with many making the most of the free drinks. The label representative from the UK division of Mercury Records was the evening's MC. Introducing all in attendance to the night, she stated she had the only advance copy available of the album in her hands, to which we would all be listening to in full on playback. A visual promo then flickered onto the screen before the album playback began.

My first impressions upon the initial listen were that it was a blending of old and new Metallica, though sound wise it was a departure, oozing with a strong garage-y sound throughout, the drums dominating proceedings, with the music heavy on the guitar riffage, and, unusual for a Metallica album, there were no guitar solos! Metallica sounded to me like they were aiming at the nu-metal market. Two hours later the evening came to an end. We were all rewarded with a sweetener, a special double CD Greatest Hits package featuring some of the band's best tunes.

Seven years later I finally got to meet the band and

interviewed Metallica lead guitarist Kirk Hammett in person in September 2010. At the time the band was in the midst of their *World Magnetic* Tour, and this 20-date leg saw them back on our shores after a six-year absence.

As one of a select few media personnel who had been granted interview access to Metallica on a very cold Wednesday afternoon, I kept this in mind, going over the questions I was going to ask as I made my way to Rod Laver Arena for my face-to-face interview with Kirk Hammett. With strict instructions from the band's people, I was told upon my arrival to wait outside by the side stage entrance for the band's Australian record label promotions person to meet me so they could usher me in. As I waited a number of die-hard Metallica fans, wearing their band's regalia, were already gathered eagerly waiting for the gate to open. As the doors finally opened they charged through rushing to get as close to the stage as possible. The night's show made it three months since Metallica had last been on stage and six years since their last Australian tour, where I saw them for the first time performing at the Sidney Myer Music Bowl in Melbourne. Tonight's show was also the first of a series of Australian shows spread out over the next couple of months.

Around 5.30pm the Universal Records rep finally escorted me into venue. Once inside I observed a group of other media people being chaperoned into the side stage door for their interviews. I walked down a long narrow corridor with adjoining side rooms along its perimeter. I was instructed to wait there until the proceeding interview had ended. There were heaps of record and tour personnel waiting around in the corridor busily moving to and fro. There was definitely a hive of activity, with numerous interviews in the adjoining rooms all in progress. As I waited,

Dino Cazares from industrial metallers Fear Factory, who were the support act for the night, along with another band The Sword, were casually hanging about in the backstage area. I had interviewed him several times over the course of his career in person, so we spoke for a few minutes. Cazares was one of those characters that provided you with memorable and hilarious interview moments. The first time I'd interviewed him was at Fear Factory's record label offices in 2001 around the time of the release of their fourth studio album *Digimortal* during which Cazares spent the entire interview answering my questions surrounded by models and playing around with a water pistol! Another time he told me a crazy moment he experienced on stage early on his career during the 1990s when Fear Factory were on tour with Ozzy Osbourne. "At the time we were touring in support of *Demanufacture* (1995) [the band's second studio album] and it was the first time we were playing really big places, that night we were playing San Diego and I had invited my family members out to see me play. And here I was rocking out onstage when suddenly the button on my shorts popped open, and down went my shorts. Now I don't wear underwear when onstage and so there was my cock hangin' out on the bottom of my guitar and here was my family watching it all!"

After Cazares had left Metallica bass player Robert Trujillo walked down the corridor having just finished his interview, followed by a popular TV presenter from a video hits show who was being escorted to a room to interview with Metallica's lead vocalist and guitarist James Hetfield. Trujillo and the band's drummer Lars Ulrich continued going about their business moving from room to room and readying themselves for the night's performance.

With the interviews on schedule, I was soon ushered

into another small room with an adjoining en suite toilet, which almost felt like a hotel room. I waited for several minutes for Hammett to arrive. When he finally surfaced, we were introduced, took our seats and I began the interview. I'd only been allocated fifteen minutes due to their hectic schedule, so did not waste any questions and we covered a lot of ground in that time. Hammett – his long curly hair tinged with specks of grey the only signs of his aging – was quietly spoken and polite, a total contrast to the public persona of one of metal's highly regarded six-string masters.

One of the questions I asked him was about the group's conscious effort to record all their live shows. "For the last ten years or so we have been recording all of our shows," Hammett confirmed, "but this EP was compiled together from a lot of different recordings. Some come from bootleg recordings that were traded on the circuits and some were recordings that are from a taping section where we'd invite people to come to the show and tape it, some of those tracks are culled from those particular recordings, and then some of it is also stuff that we had in our own recording archive."

Later that evening, Metallica performed a strong 18 song set to their legion of fans that took in tracks spanning eight different Metallica albums over the course of their career.

11 - HIRED GUNS

As a musician, finding employment as a 'hired gun' for a recording and touring artist can be quite lucrative. While many hired guns also have their own bands, as is the case with famed LA session supremo Steve Lukather who is a founding member and guitarist for the commercially successful Grammy Award winning band TOTO, side-men gigs, whether part of a touring artist's backing band or as a studio session musician, provides a doorway to unlimited possibilities both musically and professionally.

While job security may not be at the top of the list, as it can be a revolving door of players and one is never indispensable in this line of work, the benefits far outweigh the disadvantages. For instance, a musician will get paid whether the show is in a theatre or a stadium, whether it's half empty or sold-out and some of them may be paid a retainer in between tours and they also get an inside look at the inner workings of the artists themselves, and on many occasions, are brought into the artist's inner circle or 'family' so to speak.

American multi-instrumentalist Brian Ray is a prime example. Since 2002 he has been Paul McCartney's right hand man, his side-man role taking in guitar and bass playing for the former Beatle, a role he cherishes not only for the musical aspects but because McCartney has shared many personal stories that most will never get hear about. When I interviewed Ray back in 2005 he told me one of his favourite McCartney stories from his time with The

Beatles. "Paul and John [Lennon] had just finished writing their newest song called 'She Loves You' in Liverpool" said Ray, "and Paul's father had been out for the day and when he returned home, the boys had just finished writing the song. So Paul asked his father whether he would like to hear it so they start singing it for his father; 'she loves you, yeah, yeah, yeah.' Paul asks his father what he thought. And his father replied, 'It's very good Paul, but I think there is enough American-isms in the vernacular right now. Why don't you consider changing it to "she loves you, yes, yes, yes…"'!

Another important element in being a side-man is the fact that they must leave their egos at home. A side-man is there to support and enhance an artist's music and performance and those that do the touring circuit may spend many months, and in some cases years, on the road which can also affect their personal lives especially when it comes to relationships.

I've been fortunate to meet and interview a number of side-men, both from the studio and those on the touring circuit. The following are just four of my favourite moments with guitarist players Adrian Belew, Steve Lukather, Larry Carlton and keyboardist Yves Frulla. Belew has been a hired gun for bands such as Talking Heads, Joe Cocker, Nine Inch Nails, Laurie Anderson, Frank Zappa and his most well-known side-man gig with David Bowie. Bowie's '*Stage*' (1978) and '*Lodger'(1979)* albums both featured Belew's extraordinary, uniquely emotive and manipulative guitar style. Aside from his side-man gigs, he's a respected solo artist in his own right – Belew has now released around twenty solo albums to date – and is also guitarist forb influential art-rockers King Crimson. He is nicknamed 'The Rhino King', the result of the simulated sounds of the rhinoceros' grazes and snorts that appear throughout the title track of his debut solo album, *The Lone Rhino* (1981). Free form jazz-rocker Frank Zappa plucked him from obscurity at the age 27 when he saw him playing in a biker bar in Nashville and onto the world stage. In April 2006 Belew toured Australia for the very first time as a solo artist. His last tour down under had been in November 1978 with David Bowie. On the day I met him Belew was running late for sound check due to his flight from Sydney having been delayed. We were scheduled to meet at the venue – The Corner Hotel, a popular inner city pub cum live music venue that also houses a rooftop bar - at 4pm but he didn't arrive for another hour or so.

When he finally arrived with his tour manager and backing band, they all looked a little tired, but by the time I interviewed him, Belew had become more alert and refreshed. While his band and crew set-up the gear for his show, Belew looked more like a University lecturer than a musician. The dressing room was just large enough to accommodate about half a dozen musicians, and its walls were lined with tour posters from years gone by, it smelled of old cigarette smoke, had a sticky carpet - many bands old and new had all passed through its doors. Due to its close proximity to the stage, Belew's drummer and bassist could be heard sound checking through the walls. I found Belew pleasant, gentle and he told some fascinating stories. Asked about his approach to guitar playing, he answered, "to create interesting sounds and colours".

His eyes lit up when we began talking about guitars, so much so that he paused for a moment and pulled out a prototype Parker Fly he was currently using on the tour and began detailing everything about it. He revealed it had six paint finishes and that it was as light as a feather and he also told me the guitar never went out of tune. Ever! The colour he called "Turquoise Belew" and he invited me to have a play to see what I thought of it. So I picked up the guitar and proceeded to play it. It was an amazing instrument, very sleek, and definitely light compared to the weight of a normal electric guitar. The tremolo arm was amazing as no matter how hard I pulled on it or how extreme its use, it stayed in tune.

Once the stage set-up was ready Belew went ahead and sound-checked with the rhythm section which comprised a drummer and bassist. Fitting in with Belew's unorthodox playing style, the bass player played a Chapman Stick, a ten-string giant fretboard looking polyphonic instrument, the sort made famous by Tony Levin back in the '80s and not the standard fare used by most mainstream bass players. Afterwards Belew opted to make a quick dash back to his hotel room to eat and change. Once the doors opened soon after, I made my way to check out the support act. Belew finally came on stage at around 10pm and although the venue wasn't full, there was a decent turnout, most of whom were musicians. Starting the evening's set off with 'Writing On The Wall' (off his 2005 *Side One* solo album), Belew proceeded to demonstrate his amazing playing skills and the trademark noises for which he had become renowned to the extent that he had earned the title of "the stunt guitarist". He closed the evening with encore 'Thela Hun Ginjeet', a track off King Crimson's 1981 album, *Discipline.*

The following month American outfit TOTO visited our shores as part of the Australian leg of their *Falling In Between* World Tour which was brief and sold-out. Having previously started out as top notch LA studio session players, they formed in 1977 naming themselves after the dog in the 1939 film, *Wizard Of Oz*. Focusing on their virtuoso musicianship, they hit commercial and critical pay dirt with their multi Grammy award winning fourth album 1982's *Toto IV*. Steve Lukather was one of the most sought-after guitarists during the 1970s and 1980s with his guitar work appearing on over 1,500 albums during the course of his career, making him one of the most recorded musicians in the world. The band has always been, and remains, a musician's band. I had interviewed Lukather on numerous occasions during the proceeding years. He was always unafraid to speak his mind, always outspoken particularly when it came Toto and musicianship. But the 2006 tour finally allowed me the opportunity to meet him in person. It had been fourteen years since Toto had last toured the country. Unfortunately, due to the fact their Friday night show at The Palace clashed with my own band's gig the same night, I wouldn't be able to see the show, but meeting him certainly made up for it in more ways than one.

He was staying at the Grand Hyatt and we greeted each other warmly having struck up a long-distance relationship following many phone conversations down the years. Sporting a goatee Lukather gave me a welcoming hug, and in his thick American accent told everyone present that I was 'his Australian friend'. We then proceeded to the elevator to go to meet the rest of the band who were doing interviews and enjoying the Melbourne afternoon. Everything was in a relaxed and laid back mood as the day had been allocated as an official day off, though promotional duties were to be attended to.

Once we were seated, the band's label person offered Lukather some Heineken beer and he obliged. Lukather had spent many years on the booze and a few years later finally decided to quit. I actually received a letter from him a few years after our meeting apologising for his past actions, this kind of generic letter is part and parcel of the Alcoholics Anonymous recovery program. Once inside the room the whole band were enjoying themselves with drinks aplenty and sweets galore. A television film crew was present and preparing to record a live interview with the band. In the meantime, as the crew prepared, I conducted my interview with Lukather during which he expressed his undying love for The Beatles and credited them as the reason he became a musician in the first place. "I started playing when I was seven and The Beatles were it, man, it began with them," adding that over the course of his career he had the honour of working with Paul McCartney and jammed with George Harrison on Beatle tunes with Bob Dylan. We also discussed the many disputes that continued to linger between Toto and their record label with Lukather stating that, "Everybody at some point in their career has been ripped off. It is all part of the business. If you haven't been ripped off then you haven't been in the business long enough". Lukather's session background, especially with jazz musicians, tended to inform a lot of his vocabulary, for example whenever he talked about other musicians, he referred to them as 'cats'. Once completed, he re-joined the rest of the band who were now all seated on a couch in front of the cameras and ready for action.

With the TV presenter seated in the middle of the band, the members gave such an hilarious interview, humour which permeated throughout the band's personnel, which began the moment the host introduced the band, by welcoming them back to Australia. They responded by breaking out in song, a cappella style with 'Welcome Back' the theme to 1970s sitcom *Welcome Back, Kotter*, before Toto vocalist Bobby Kimball interrupted by saying,

"I've never been here!" At one point during the interview Lukather picked up his sunglasses and placed them on upside down which caused much laughter once again. Greg Phillinganes, the newest member to join the band just the year prior, was jokingly referred to by Lukather as the 'black Jerry Lewis' to which Phillinganes proceeded to live up to that name by performing some hilarious Lewis-style skits. Topics covered in the television interview ranged from the band now being an indie band, to when they would be returning to Australia, which Lukather had told me earlier in my interview would be around February next year – they would eventually return in March 2008 – and this time with more shows and cities added to the tour schedule. After the interview, as we wrapped things up for the day, Lukather invited me to the band's sound check the following day, but I had to decline due to my own band's schedule.

Between 1970 and 1977 American guitarist Larry Carlton was one of the most in-demand LA session guitarists on the scene, performing on more than 3,000 studio sessions. The studio session supremo's guitar playing has appeared on hundreds of albums from artists as revered as Steely Dan, Michael Jackson, Neil Diamond, Leo Sayer and Christopher Cross to name but a few. His blistering guitar solo on Steely Dan's 'Kid Charlemagne' from their 1976 *The Royal Scam* became the defining Carlton moment, so much so that *Rolling Stone* called it 'one of three greatest rock guitar solos ever'. He eventually quit session work in 1977 to forge a solo career – his unique blend of jazz fusion and pop influences proved so popular that he has been releasing albums ever since. He also miraculously survived a near-fatal shooting near his Burbank studio in 1987.

In April 2007 Carlton visited Australia for the first time. He is known as Mr. 335 – so named due to his signature use of the Gibson ES-335 guitar and I was slated to interview him before he played a show with fellow American blues-jazz guitarist Robben Ford that evening. Softly spoken, bespectacled and with thinning hair we chatted but I quickly found that any answers relating to past achievements were brief while his replies to my questions relating to his current projects received lengthier answers. Carlton definitely preferred not to dwell on his past and I understood his reasoning. Usually, whenever artists embark on promotional duties it's due to wanting to promote their latest work, tour or project. But with such a respected musical background and body of work, it's hard not to delve a little. Also the manner of how an interviewer asks a question is an integral part in the type of answer received and whether that artist opens up or does not reveal much.

For example, when I asked him about 'Kid Charlemagne', his reply was curt: "that was thirty years ago", before adding, "I can't remember". Immediately, sensing his hesitation in discussing the past, I changed tack which allowed a connection to occur between us, from that moment on he opened up and answered my questions a lot more in-depth and with interest. For example, when I asked him how important to him those early session years were in regards to his later solo career, he replied; "It taught me how to make records and it was great exposure that helped shape my playing". Before revealing, "When I eventually quit doing sessions in 1977, it was not because I wanted a solo career, but because I was so busy for all those seven years that I couldn't charge any more money and I couldn't take any more work, as the session scene was already at the peak of what could be had".

In April 2008 I was given the opportunity to go behind the scenes on Celine Dion's Australian tour. Part of the assignment was to interview Yves Frulla, Dion's touring keyboardist, who would provide me with a bird's eye view of all the happenings behind the scenes. The classically-trained pianist first joined Dion's band in 1990 as part of her *Unison Canadian* tour. As I made my way into Melbourne the day turned out to be quite chaotic, as a gale ripped through the city, with almost blizzard like conditions. Many suburbs ended up losing power and traffic became chaotic, taking hours to get through on the roads, and so it was quite a stressful drive. I finally arrived at Rod Laver Arena very late in the afternoon and made my way backstage. A number of semi-trailers and several large vans that carried the gear and crew were all lined up beside the entrance.

Celine Dion was originally scheduled to perform the previous night but a week earlier many of the Australian dates on her *Taking Chances* tour were rescheduled due to her coming down with a minor throat infection and irritated sinuses. So the previous evening's show in Melbourne had to be reshuffled to this evening. Her first stop on the tour had been in Brisbane.

Frulla was waiting for me outside the door of the backstage entrance of the arena and after a quick handshake and greeting, he ushered me into the backstage area. Though Frulla's strong voice was tinged with a slight French accent, he had a good command of English and spoke elegantly. He handed me my AAA pass, then quickly escorted me to the stage area as the band was due onstage in a few minutes time to begin sound checking. He quickly took me for a tour of the stage and how the show operated. As he was showing me round he introduced me to various other members of the band particularly the two guitarists; André Coutu and Jean Sebastien Carré (who also played violin).

Two drum kits were set up onstage within a plexiglass wall and, although a selection of guitars were onstage, the amps and speaker cabinets were carefully placed backstage hidden away from the audience. Most of the other crew seemed to be French speaking.

I was curious to ask him how long they'd spend in pre-tour rehearsals. "Not that much" he revealed before continuing, "for this tour it has been very little. We first rehearsed the band for four weeks in a rehearsal hall and put all the music together. Then we went into an arena and did three weeks of production with all the stage set-ups and video stuff and we rehearsed with everything together. Then we went to South Africa and did a couple rehearsals over there and from there we started the current world tour. But the tour has evolved already, as a lot of the stuff we put together in the rehearsal is no longer there. We always have to adjust quickly because there are always requests. I do a lot of music programming in my hotel room and some software because I always need to come up with some stuff while we're on tour. So, we experiment with set list changes and stuff all the time".

As the band took their places on stage and prepared to kick off the sound check, Yves asked me to take a seat anywhere I liked. Because the venue had placed seating in the floor area in front of the stage, I decided to take my seat up front, so I had the best view possible. The band ran through each instrument first in order to check individual sound and volume levels, then ran through a couple of songs such as cover of 'Alone' by Heart which sounded great even without Dion's vocals. The cover saw Andre playing an emotive classical guitar line before charging into the chorus with some ripping power chords. The production was very slick and big.

An hour passed and Dion had yet to turn up for sound check, so the band just waited around and jammed on a few things. In the meantime, I asked Andre if he ever played an Australian made Maton acoustic. He told me that he had never heard of them so I told him more about them. I noticed they played Takamine acoustics, and a selection of other electric guitars comprised mainly of Gibson Les Pauls and a couple of cool Fender Stratocasters. Then one of Dion's entourage came up to me, advised me that Dion was about to enter the stage so instructed me to 'move away from front of stage' as Dion didn't like having anyone in the vicinity of the stage while she was on there. I was told no photos were to be taken. I obliged and moved to another location where I was hidden from view and Dion finally emerged. It had just gone 6.15pm. She had a male chauffeur with her and was in a loose fitting dress, wearing high heels and looked very casual. She joked around with band members, even throwing some very unwomanly like moves. It was quite hilarious to watch in fact, and showed a different side to her public persona. She spoke mostly in French for the entire time and as she sang the songs, her voice echoed across the arena. It sounded majestic. It was effortless, natural and pure. She kicked off with 'Chain', an old soul number, and then ran through a few other songs that showcased her versatility. At one point she grabbed some tissues and blew her nose, which obviously showed that her cold was still to some extent there but you could hardly tell from her singing. About 45 minutes later the sound check was finally declared over. Dion, together with her entourage, quickly departed back stage.

With doors scheduled to open soon, Frulla quickly asked me if I had any more questions to ask and I replied that I had one more. Having just witnessed the sound check I was curious to find out more about how Dion approached her sound checks. "Obviously we don't have much time to sound check, so we work extremely fast as Celine is not a person who likes to rehearse a lot so we have to keep up with her all the time. Usually the main thing is to make sure that the front of house mix is okay. So, we go through different styles of songs where we can get either an up-tempo or ballad something in order to get different frequencies so the guy at the front can establish his mix. And then when Celine gets in, we make sure her headphone mix is solid because even though it's a headphone mix, every venue changes because her microphone picks up a lot so it can change for her. We have to make sure that in the time that we have, that her mix is good. She is the star and she needs to sing and the front of house guy has to be happy. The rest we just get to go, which is why we do all the work in pre-production where we establish all the setup and make sure it's okay right down to the minute changes".

As a footnote in 2015 Frulla, along with guitarist Coutu, violinist Carré and band-leader Claude "Mégo" Lemay, were all fired by Dion's management. The laconic official press release making the firings public stated that Dion wanted "…to give new life to the show".

12 - EMO KIDS

The birth of what has been labelled 'emo' – short for 'emotional' - can be traced back to the middle part of the 1980s when the genre arose out of the post-hardcore punk scene in Washington D.C. Its influence soon spread over to the west coast of the United States where it finally began to evolve with a strong emphasis on expressing the individual's experiences of pain and loss, along with emotional and often confessional lyrical subject matter, resonating with a generation of teenagers. Spreading further afield across to the American mid-west in the post grunge 1990s, it was further refined into the form it became most widely known for. On through the new millennia and the 2000s the genre rode a wave of popularity in the hands of bands such as My Chemical Romance, The Used, Taking Back Sunday, Jimmy Eat World, The Get Up Kids, Fall Out Boy and Dashboard Confessional.

In October 2005 I met up for a face-to-face interview with Quinn Allman, one of the founding members and guitarist with The Used who were then riding hiding. The band was in town as part of the *Taste Of Chaos* package tour, a new live music extravaganza that had started that year in the United States and expanded into other territories including Australia. The tour catered for a younger generation of music fans who were into genres such as emo, metal core and pop-punk. *Taste of Chaos* afforded bands such as The Used, who were the headliners on this inaugural trek, a platform to reach their intended audience on a mass scale.

With all the bands on the Australian leg of *Taste Of Chaos* in town and undertaking promotional duties I was granted a half hour with Allman and The Used lead vocalist Bert McCracken at their hotel room. The band had released their second album *In Love and Death* a year prior, and it proved to be their most commercially successful to date so the band were still touring in support of it.

With his heavily tattooed arms, long dark bleached hair and a beer in hand, McCracken was, at that time, going through a dark time personally, dealing with the aftermath of the tragic death of his pregnant girlfriend to a drug overdose the year before. Despite his personal circumstances and the huge emotional load he was carrying, I found him very open and happy to discuss whatever questions were put to him regardless of the subject matter which included discussing his documented battles with drug addiction and his love affair with Kelly Osbourne. I sensed that having these type of conversations, especially when life on the road could be hard and lonely at times, helped bring him some sort of catharsis, and possibly helped in his healing process. Allman, on the other hand, was very reserved and showed no interest in the interview. And though he occasionally did join in to add his two cents worth into the conversation, he spent most of our interview time gazing out of the hotel room window, all the while smoking a cigarette and taking sips of beer.

The Used's back story was a fairy tale of sorts. Members of the band had experienced homelessness, drug addiction and constantly fought with a rebellious spirit against the mentality of small Mormon town in Orem, Utah. Their determination to succeed on their own terms saw the band achieve acceptance within the emo and punk circles, gradually building a solid fan base that saw their audience grow bigger with each show, even though their media profile was still non-existent.

The band's previous Australian tour earlier that same year had seen the 2,000 tickets for their Sydney show sell-out in just five minutes and with that demand came the need to move the original show to a larger venue of over 5,000 which also sold-out in an hour. All of this was accomplished purely through word of mouth and their strong fan base was mostly comprised of young females. It was all done without the support of major radio or media too. Quite an achievement in itself and showed the popularity of not only the band, but of the emo genre.

By the time I next met up with the band, about eighteen months later in May 2007, the genre had reached its peak and would soon begin to wane. This time I was allocated time with just Allman himself. This meeting was a stark contrast compared to the Allman I had met previously. On this occasion the interview occurred at the band's Australian record label Warner Music which was operating out of a multi-storey late Victorian terrace house in the inner northern Melbourne suburb of Carlton.

The band were in town for their own shows touring in support of their recently released third studio album, *Lies For The Liars*. Arriving for the scheduled late afternoon interview, I was escorted by the band's publicist to a spacious downstairs room where the interview and asked to take a seat while Allman finished up an interview in another room on the upper floor. The room was adorned by various block mounts of album covers on its walls. These included numerous Warner artists such as Madonna and The Cure. Beneath them sat rows of wooden units each with pigeon holes that were overflowing with CDs stored and each addressed to respective music magazine, television and radio personnel for promotional post outs. A giant wooden desk and stylish leather swivel chair took prime position in the room, from where the publicist undertook their daily duties.

Allman, wearing a white striped polo shirt and now sporting a toothbrush moustache, eventually arrived, greeted me and took his seat behind the desk. He turned to me and jokingly remarked as if he was the label head and I was an applicant applying for a position in his company;

"This is the boss's seat, so what can you bring to this company?"

"Well, I can bring my expertise and knowledge" I replied, to which he added, "I do have a perfectionist streak..."

It was a hilarious way to break the ice. This was a different Allman to the one I met previously, where he had sat in the corner lost in his thoughts as he gazed out the hotel window. I thought it was really weird at the time and wondered why he displayed such disinterest, but on this occasion I came to the realization that he was actually just shy.

I had been advised by the publicist that no questions were to be asked or any discussions undertaken about the rift that had occurred between The Used and fellow emo rockers My Chemical Romance. Both bands had paired up and recently recorded and released a cover of Queen's 1981 classic 'Under Pressure', but they had subsequently fallen out and relations between the bands had become frozen. As two of the most popular bands on the emo scene, this was headline news for the music press. The publicist advised that McCracken, who was doing interviews at another location, had grown tired of constantly being asked about the rift, feeling the press were more interested in the fall out rather than the band's music. Allman was much more relaxed and attentive this time and happily answered all my questions, fully engaging in the conversation. He sat comfortably with a glass of champagne in his hand. Due to the band needing to head out for their sound check at Festival Hall for their show later that evening, I was only allocated fifteen minutes, though the interview went well and proved very productive. The Used returned to Australia again later that same year for another round of *The Taste Of Chaos* tour.

New Jersey outfit My Chemical Romance were always regarded as the titular head of the emo scene, yet the band fought constantly against any kind of labelling. With influences that ranged from The Misfits to Iron Maiden and from Morrissey to Queen and beyond, the band always believed their music had more to offer than what the emo movement stood for. As guitarist Ray Toro told me, "If that's what people want to call us, then that's fair enough. I've come to the conclusion that people will say what they want to say". As their 2006 sprawling concept album *The Black Parade* confirmed, the band's influences were very diverse with everything from glam rock to vaudeville thrown into the mix.

The band had first toured Australia as one of the opening acts on Green Day's *American Idiot* Stadium Tour in December 2005. My Chemical Romance toured the country again in January and February of 2007 as part of the *Big Day Out* festival which is when I caught up with them. As was the usual *modus operandi* for me I arrived nice and early in time for my 6pm interview time. A small group of the band's diehard fans had already gathered outside the hotel with cameras and posters in hand, in the hope of catching a glimpse of their idols and due to the band's popularity with the emo kids, security stood guard outside each of the band members' hotel rooms. We were ushered into one of the rooms and told to wait and remain quiet as one of the band members was in the middle of an interview. Shortly thereafter, a group of twenty-somethings with a film crew in tow were following the group's lead singer Gerard Way, who was trying unsuccessfully to disguise himself with a hooded sweatshirt, walked past us in the hotel's corridor, and continued on their way until they reached his hotel room. It was apparent that the film crew were filming some sort of 'on the road' documentary.

Toro, with a mop of black hair and dressed all in black, greeted me warmly and although he answered my questions openly, I noticed he hardly made eye contact and looked away whenever he answered. I sensed it was more to do with shyness than anything else, as toward the end of our interview, as he began to feel more comfortable, he began looking me more confidently in the eye.

Shyness and introversion is a very common trait among musicians and performers. This surprises many in the general public as their perception of the favourite artists is largely formed by their showmanship before an audience. With many utilizing outlandish stage personas or lavish stage shows, they're perceived as being extroverts or even narcissists yet nothing could be further from the truth. Nearly every artist or musician I've met tends to harbour this 'shyness' trait. One of the most famous and well known shy performers was the late, great David Bowie. The many personas he adopted during the 1970s such as Ziggy Stardust (an androgynous rock star and intergalactic messenger) and The Thin White Duke (a gaunt, fascist aristocrat) were nothing more than characters that would allow him to act out his need to be extrovert onstage, a mask of sorts in order to be able to do what he did best: perform and sing. Bowie confirmed his shyness and introvert nature in several interviews he did over the course of his career.

My interview with Toro turned out to be the last one for the band on the day, as the band were about to head out for their sound check after which they would have dinner and then perform their headlining side-show later in the evening at Festival Hall. After the show, the band would take a couple days off before heading off onto their next stop over in Adelaide as part of the *Big Day Out* run of shows.

Taking Back Sunday's sound is best described as a cocktail of emo, hardcore and pop-punk. Like all bands their sound has evolved and matured over the years but those elements were what first captured my attention when I came across the band's music in the early 2000s. In March 2006 I was given the opportunity to catch up with them when they were in town for their very first tour down under. The tour itself saw sold-out shows for the band in most cities around the country and in Melbourne, both their under 18 and 18 and over shows were sold out too. The band were about to release their major label debut *Louder Now* (their third album) come April, after they had signed with Warner Music the year prior. Their previous releases were all on Victory Records and both albums, *Where You Want To Be* (2004) and *Tell All Your Friends* (2002) had recently been accredited Gold status in the U.S.

I met the band at the Marquee Hotel in the beach side suburb of St Kilda. The hotel has been quite a popular place for visiting international music acts in Melbourne. I interviewed many music artists at this hotel over years. I

Interviewing Taking Back Sunday's Fred Mascherino and Eddie Reyes in October, 2006 in Melbourne.

was there to interview Taking Back Sunday's two guitaists Fred Mascherino, who played lead, and the band's main stay Eddie Reyes who played rhythm. They greeted me warmly in the hotel lobby upon my arrival before we made our way to the restaurant. It was already mid-afternoon, and the place was a buzz of activity as afterwards they'd be heading out on their way to perform their special under 18s afternoon show that would see the band hitting the stage at 5pm. We took our seats and spent the next half hour talking about the new album, guitars and life on the road and some of their guilty pleasures which for Reyes involved watching loads of old school horror flicks. He was wearing a *Dawn of The Dead* t-shirt, and told me that George Romero was one of his favourite horror movie makers. I also met the tour manager Ward who was also a great guy, and who had been very helpful in making sure everything was running smoothly. Unfortunately the record label had sent me a sampler of the album only a few days prior and on the day of my interview, it still had not arrived. So on the morning of my interview I had to jump online to seek out what I could find about the new album, and listen to their current single, 'MakeDamnSure' from it, so that I had a decent indication of what the rest of the album would sound like.

After the interview I headed straight to the Hi-Fi Bar on scenic Swanston Street, where the band was performing their show. As I made my way through the venue, it was literally swarming with teeny boppers, with many of the girls already in hysterics as the band began performing their set. I secured a spot near the front and watched the show. A group of girls managed to find their way to the front of the stage and handed the band a large plastic kangaroo which the band tied to their monitors where it would remain for the whole show. Seeing that their gift was now given centre stage attention, the girls went crazy with excitement and launched into deafening screams of joy. The group's vocalist, Adam Lazzara, threw them further into hysterics, when he kept swinging his microphone cable from side to side, reminiscent of the young Golden God himself Robert Plant. Lazzara was the supreme emo-pop poster boy!

The show confirmed without a doubt that Taking Back Sunday had an enormous bright future ahead of them. With this kind of audience response and devotion, I knew we were going to be hearing lots more from the band in future.

The band returned to Australia that October and again I was dispatched to interview Mascherino and Reyes again. The band were there as part of the *Taste Of*

Chaos tour, with their show later that evening at Vodafone Arena. It would see Taking Back Sunday joined on the bill by the aforementioned The Used, Thursday, Senses Fail, Underoath and others. As I wandered into the luxurious hotel foyer to wait for my contact from Warner Music, Mascherino happened to casually stroll inside. Instantly recognizing me from our last interview, he greeted me and we shook hands. We struck up an enjoyable conversation and he kindly gave me some wonderful feedback on our last interview which had been published for a guitar website. Before our interview though, he informed me that he had to go and do another interview before mine, so he excused himself and off he went to do that. That interview saw him being interviewed alongside bassist Matt Rubano and was being filmed by a video crew, possibly for a TV broadcast.

As this was going on I made my way to the outside courtyard at the back of the hotel and took a seat near the pool. A young couple were sunbathing nearby enjoying the scenery whilst also being privy to the band's interviews. Life didn't get any better than that. Here I was interviewing a couple of rock stars on a beautiful, sunny Melbourne day next to the spacious confines of the hotel's swimming pool – it was like a scene out of a Hollywood movie.

After they had finished their interview, Mascherino came over and brought up the subject of our last interview and said how much he enjoyed talking to me. Reyes concurred and told me that he remembered our last chat. They told me that since that earlier interview back in March the past six months had been very hectic for the band. Their major label debut *Louder Now* had debuted at number 2 on the US Billboard charts and with the constant touring and headlining appearances, the band's profile had risen considerably. We had another great chat while one of the band's crew filmed our interview, which I assume would either had been for the band's own keep sake or possibly for material to be used at a later date such as a DVD release. I never did find out if it got used.

Success hadn't spoiled Reyes and Mascherino as I found both were just as down to earth as they had been the first time we had met. Both were still as passionate about music, totally genuine human beings with a warmth about them that was very welcoming. Mascherino always had a smile on his face along with an infectious happy-go-lucky attitude. In fact, he and I got along so well we remained in contact over the years. He eventually played a brilliant guitar solo on one of my instrumental tracks 'Endless Summer' that I released in 2012 on my solo album *Creature Of Habit*. It was an honour to have him play on it.

Both mentioned that with the tight *Taste Of Chaos* schedule they wouldn't have time to savour the delights of Melbourne, having only arrived earlier that day. With more interviews scheduled for that afternoon, then the show that night, they'd be leaving for the airport the next day for the next show in Sydney.

After our interview I wished them the best for their show, Mascherino in turn wished the best for my band's show later that night. One of the festival organizers had granted me a quick tour of the workings of the tour backstage, so before departing I raced over to Vodafone Arena. Hundreds of teenyboppers largely dressed in black, with side swept hairdos were already lined up outside the venue ready for the 5pm opening. I entered through the backstage load-in area where several semi-trailers were parked having been unloaded of gear earlier. A number of the crew were out and about undertaking their duties while security manned the entrances on all sides. One of the festival's tour managers escorted me through the vast complex and onto the bands' communal hospitality room where an abundance of food and drink lined the makeshift tables. Several members from some of the bands were gathered around the tables chatting away, while others were tapping away on their laptops or phones. Along the corridors rooms had been designated for each band with their respective names clearly marked on each door. All the bands on the tour bill had their bags and belongings tucked away in the rooms where most would be used as changing rooms later on as well.

The following year, in late 2007, Fred Mascherino left Taking Back Sunday to concentrate on his band The Color Fred. It was later revealed that tensions within Taking Back Sunday had been ongoing for a while, and when I caught up again with him after his exit from the band in 2007 I asked him why he left, he told me, "I didn't leave the band simply to do this [The Color Fred] I left the band because I felt it had hit the end of the road. We were trying to write our fourth record and the excitement that I had writing the last two just wasn't there for me. And it really showed because when we were writing *Louder Now*, we had got together and in the first week we came out with four of the songs. But when we were writing for the new record, we couldn't finish one song and we had been at it for months".

Mascherino went on to form another band, Terrible Things, which released their self-titled debut in 2010. I finally met up with him again in 2011 when the band toured Australia to perform shows as part of the Counter Revolution festival, an offshoot of the annual Sound Wave Festival, the Counter Revolution was a mini-festival which was lucky to still go ahead after it encountered numerous problems during its planning stages. Starting out as Soundwave Revolution with Van Halen set to headline before later pulling out, the festival had to be moved twice in Melbourne before ending up at Festival Hall with a fraction of the original line-up still playing. Other cities also had their venues downgraded to accommodate a smaller than expected turn out. Melbourne's show was shifted from an outdoor venue and with around 19 bands on the final bill.

I got there early in order to catch the Terrible Things set, as they were second on after the opening band. Mascherino's band played a fantastic 30 minute set, one of the best I'd seen in a long while. Even now, writing this many years later, I can still remember the brilliance of that set. I am not trying to be biased here, but honestly I have to state that everything Mascherino puts his hand to musically is masterful, second to none and timeless. I've mentioned to him many times over the years in our email correspondences how *Bend To Break* (The Color Fred album) is one of the finest albums of the 2000s.

13 - DO WHAT THOU WILT

Three-piece Canadian rock band The Tea Party first formed in Windsor, Ontario in 1990. Windsor, which sits on the Canadian side of the Detroit River which divided the metro areas of Windsor and Detroit was also home to Shania Twain one of the biggest female country-pop-rock artists of all time. Led by charismatic front man and guitarist Jeff Martin along with bassist and keyboardist Stuart Chatwood and drummer Jeff Burrows, The Tea Party quickly found favour with Australian audiences in the wake of their major label debut album *Splendor Solis* in 1993. Prior to their major label debut, they had released an eponymous debut album through their own label Eternal Discs in 1991.

Australia proved to be the first country outside of their native Canada to embrace the band wholeheartedly and their epic and unique blend of rock and world music, referred to at times as 'Moroccan Roll', that was sprinkled with flourishes of electronica. The songs' lyrical themes also weighed heavily on the occult and spiritual subject matter, the result of Martin's deep interest in esoteric philosophies that began in his late teenage years. This brought a mystique to the band which helped propel interest in their music. In October 2006 the band split acrimoniously due to differing opinions on the musical direction of the band and vowed to never work together again but five years later they reunited and continued where they had left off.

Their love affair with Australia was further etched in stone with the release the following year of the *Live From*

Australia album which was funded by their fans. The Tea Party have undertaken numerous tours of the country since the 1990s and I got to meet Jeff Martin on their Australian tour in early 2002, which saw them perform their own shows as well as appear on legs of *Big Day Out* in Adelaide and Perth. As a long time devotee of infamous British occultist Aleister Crowley, Martin has followed Crowley's mantra of, 'love is the law, love under will' to the letter both personally and musically through his life and career. Crowley was the self-proclaimed 'Great Beast 666' who had a fondness for drugs, sex magick – Crowley even added the 'k' to magic to differentiate it between the occultic practice from stage magic - esoteric writings and poetry, created his own spiritual philosophy called Thelema. Crowley's treatise 'Liber AL vel Legis' better known as *The Book Of The Law* and published in 1909, based it's central precept on 'Do what thou wilt shall be the whole of the Law'. Crowley, who adhered to a self-indulgent lifestyle, died a pauper in 1947 but years after his death his writings began to pervade popular culture and received a further boost when The Beatles placed a portrait of Crowley on their iconic *Sgt Pepper's Lonely Hearts Club Band* album cover. Others followed suit, including the likes of David Bowie and Led Zeppelin's Jimmy Page who started name checking Crowley and his works. Page even went as far as purchasing his old residence in the early 1970s. Crowley's philosophy and writings suddenly found favour again and a new home within both the esoteric circles and the music fraternity.

I first met Jeff Martin in February 2002 when the band was in town touring in support of *The Interzone Mantras*, their sixth studio album that had been released a few months earlier. This was their ninth Australian tour and it took in eleven shows. They were scheduled to perform two shows at The Palais in St. Kilda and I was on assignment from *Rolling Stone* to do a story on Martin and the band. I was issued with an AAA pass and after arriving at the venue, a couple hours before show time, I met Martin in the peaceful confines of his dressing room which was located alongside the back area of the stage. The room was one of several along a stretch of corridor that was allocated to the band and crew. The backstage was cordoned off prior to the show so that the band could prepare for the evening's performance. Martin had one room all to himself. I entered and was introduced to him by a solidly-built bodyguard who never left his side whenever Martin travelled away from the stage area. Martin greeted me in his deep resonant voice and with his dark eyes and magnetic presence, he was captivating. He was also a dead ringer for the late Doors front man Jim Morrison.

A bottle of Jack Daniels and several bottles of water and beer sat on the lighted mirror bench next to Martin. We engaged in conversation for a short while and he then told me that I should follow him back to his hotel after the evening's show where we would be able to conduct an interview. My wife Liz had been waiting for my interview to finish, and I called her to come into the venue but as she walked around trying to find the dressing room Martin and I were in, she soon got lost until she saw someone standing on the stage facing the backline. She made her way to him to ask for directions and it turned out to be Australian concert promoter Michael Gudinski who happily pointed her in the right direction. I left Martin and departed for the stage where my wife and I prepared to take our seats near Martin's guitar tech area, so that we could watch the entire show from the side of the stage.

Lined up next to the guitar tech lay multiple guitar racks that housed an array of string instruments that Martin would play during the evening's performance. The collection comprised a collection of electric guitars that included a double neck, several Gibson Les Pauls, a Fender Telecaster and an assortment of exotic instruments that included a Tanpura, an Oud and a sitar. The band was known to take over 35 instruments on tour with them. As the house lights dimmed, the band prepared to hit the stage to the roar of the audience. Each took their positions, as Martin picked up his guitar and walked to the microphone. The band kicked off the show with 'Interzone', the first track of their latest album. From then on, the band held the audience in the palm of their hand the entire evening. Martin was the master magician weaving his musical spell upon the audience, Dionysus in human form. The atmosphere in the room was electric, the energy highly charged and infectious. Each song saw a change of instrument for Martin with Chatwood also exchanging instruments on several occasions. His guitar tech was kept busy throughout the performance, preparing each instrument for each song's changeover. He tuned and restrung the guitars and made sure the switch over ran seamlessly. The band ran through a strong eighteen song set finishing up with an encore of a cover of The Rolling Stones 'Paint It Black', that blended their mix of western and eastern influences to perfection and which brought the night's proceedings to a fever pitch end. Martin and his cohorts took a bow and then, dripping in sweat and exhausted, exited the stage to the sound of loud applause. They headed straight to their respective dressing rooms to come down from the high of the night's performance. Later they made their way back to the Marriott Hotel on

Russell St where I headed for the interview.

Martin arrived back at the hotel dressed all in black, with matching leather pants and jacket accompanied by his bodyguard as he walked into the hotel's foyer which now had filled with hanger-ons, groupies and friends. Liz and I joined Martin and we commented on the night's brilliant performance. Martin and I found a couch in a quiet area of the hotel and I found him articulate, well-read and forthright. With a shared interest in esoteric philosophies, we discussed Crowley and the German philosopher Friedrich Nietzsche. Martin definitely walked the walk when it came to his interest in matters of the occult and in particular Crowley. He took his esoteric interest seriously, and when I expressed to him my growing interest in Crowley, he highly recommended to me in picking up a copy of *777 and Other Qabalistic Writings of Aleister Crowley*, which he informed me was one of the books that took pride of place in his occult library. He also expressed to me how those who claimed to understand Nietzsche, yet couldn't even pronounce his name correctly, tellingly revealed a lack of authenticity on their behalf. As our interview came to an end, I asked Martin for a photo for posterity, and asked Liz to take the photo for me. As Martin prepared to stand with me for the photo opportunity, he raised his hand and ran his fingers through his hair, looked to Liz and asked her, 'How's my hair?' With the late night hours ticking into the early morning, I thanked Martin and wished him the best for the reminder of the tour. He requested that I send him a copy of the *Rolling Stone* article once it was published.

The Tea Party returned later that same year in October to perform at the *M-ONE* festival where the band were on the same bill as fellow Canadians Nickelback as well as Goo Goo Dolls, Billy Idol, Garbage, Simple Plan and several local acts. The festival was being staged at Colonial Stadium and the night before it I had caught up with Martin again at the Grand Hyatt where I was interviewing Nickelback, as both bands were staying in the same hotel. Martin was loitering in the hotel's dining area near where members of Nickelback and I were sat deep in conversation. As soon as I noticed Martin, I excused myself and called out to him. Martin was also wearing a black and white bandanna similar to the one I was wearing. He greeted me warmly. I mentioned that the interview I had done with him earlier in the year had finally been published in *Rolling Stone* magazine that same week and was now out. Again, he had also brought along his solidly built bodyguard whom I had also met previously. Martin asked me if I could give me him a copy of the magazine and I said I'd bring it to him to the show the following day at Colonial Stadium show. He was pleased to hear that and said, 'see you then' and left with his bodyguard and crew in tow.

The next day as we arrived at the stadium I put in a call to Martin's bodyguard who informed me that due to the festival's tight schedule, nobody would be allowed backstage, and because of that, I would not be able to catch up with him. Instead the bodyguard instructed me to meet him on the stadium ground so he could grab the magazine from me personally, which we did prior to the band's set. We later watched The Tea Party set, which was great, though in a stadium setting the music lacked some of the atmospheric elements that were integral to the band's music, which their Palais show had affirmed in spades. Because of this the band played harder and more aggressively than they had previously. The added aggressive energy saw Martin breaking a lot more guitar strings during the set.

It would be another four years before I caught up with

Martin for our next meeting. In June 2006 he was in town on a promo tour behind his solo debut effort *Exile and the Kingdom*. Unfortunately in the wake of the band's tour with Def Leppard the prior year, Martin had split the band, packed his bags and taken his wife and new son with him and headed for the remote hills of Ireland. Having gone through the abuses of drink and drugs, he decided it was time to clean himself up and this new found lifestyle and life in a rural environment proved to be his saving grace. A rejuvenated Martin was showcased on his new solo outing, which to many fans sounded like the Tea Party circa *Edges of Twilight* (1995).

This time around it was a lot more subdued and Martin had no bodyguard, nor any sort of entourage bar an assistant who handled his promotional duties. We met at the very non-rock 'n' roll hour of 10am at his hotel apartment in down town Carlton, a few minutes walking distance from the heart of Melbourne. Entering his room we re-aquainted ourselves, and recalled our earlier meetings. Still looking every bit the rock star, he was elegantly and stylishly dressed and wearing snakeskin boots. While his physical attributes still reminded me of Jim Morrison, he now seemed to have more of an uncanny resemblance to early 1970s Jimmy Page and the similarities didn't end there as Page was also a lifelong acolyte of Crowley. In fact in the 1990s The Tea Party opened for Jimmy Page and Robert Plant on the pair's *No Quarter* tour where Page and Martin would engage in an exchange of their Crowley philosophies.

With a cigarette between his fingers Martin discussed his new solo album, his newly built Australian made Ellis 7 string guitar, the reason behind the split with his Tea Party band mates and of course, no interview with Martin would be complete without a mention of Crowley. Interestingly enough, Martin revealed that around the time of the band's fourth album *Transmission* (1997) he was ingesting huge amounts of illicit substances and with his predilection for Crowley's works and rituals, he had found himself in a very dark space which only recently had finally been cleansed from his psyche. He was grateful for coming out of it on the other side, and reflected that by being in a pure state and centring oneself his Crowley activities would take on a more positive role that he believed would help him walk with the light rather than the dark. This enlightenment brought about a reassessment of his life and the end of The Tea Party.

In the wake of the death of the band's manager in 2003 and unhappy with the commercial direction the band were heading on 2004's *Seven Circles* album, along with the inherent pressures on trying to crack the tough American market, Martin finally enough and decided to split the band. This led to acrimonious feelings between Martin and the other two band members. With their relationship in tatters, and business affairs needing sorting, even the band's equipment got embroiled in legalities. When I asked him about the large collection of world instruments and guitars that he had amassed whilst in the band he told me, "I had around 50 in my collection and they were gone for a while" he admitted, adding "because when Tea Party broke up all the instruments that we got over the years we'd bought as a corporation so when the band dissolved those things were in limbo. But I just finally got them all back".

While living in Ireland Martin found time to form a new three-piece outfit called The Armada. After his stint in Ireland Martin eventually emigrated to Australia, setting up home in the more laid back and Mediterranean-style climate of Perth. He also formed the power trio 777, named after his favourite Crowley book. He later relocated to the country's quintessential bohemian beachside commune of Byron Bay on Australia's eastern seaboard where he also set up his own recording studio.

14 - LEGENDS

Legend - noun, someone very famous and admired usually because of their ability in a particular field.

The Shadows are one of the most influential bands of the 20th century. Their instrumental catalogue is second to none and guitarist Hank Marvin is Britain's most influential guitar player, and was the first real guitar hero of an entire generation, themselves in turn influential. Ritchie Blackmore, Eric Clapton, Jeff Beck, Brian May, Pete Townshend, David Gilmour, Mark Knopfler all cite Marvin as the reason they first started playing guitar. With the bespectacled Marvin and his trademark Fiesta Red Stratocaster at the helm, The Shadows, who started out as Cliff Richard's backing band in 1958, went on to score hit after hit with their instrumental fare. Their signature instrumental, 'Apache' topped the UK charts for five weeks in 1960. They were one of the most popular music outfits on the British music scene until the emergence of The Beatles.

When I first picked up the guitar in 1981 one of the albums that I now consider my "guitar school" was The Shadows *20 Golden Greats* which was released in 1977. I first bought it on cassette and spent months learning to play guitar from it. It proved to be one of the most influential moments of my musical life. So imagine my surprise when twenty-six years later in August of 2007 I was given the opportunity to finally meet Marvin. He had emigrated to Australia in 1986 and had lived in Perth ever since but this interview took place at the offices of Universal Music in Melbourne. In all the years of doing music journalism up to that point, this was the first time I'd actually been in the Universal Music building. I had been numerous times to other labels in town from Sony to Warner but Universal seemed to somehow elude me. Previously, I'd mostly done Universal artists interviews either on the phone or face-to-face with the artists in their hotel rooms or backstage.

Upon arrival, I was informed by reception that the publicist who was chauffeuring Marvin from place to place was running late. With most of the label's people working away upstairs, I decided to take a look around the reception area where block mounts of some of the label's most popular artists hung on the walls. In front of me and right above the couch I was sitting on sat a signed portrait of Scissor Sisters that each member had autographed and signed to "Universal Melbourne Thanks". Others such as Sting, Eminem and Metallica were spaced evenly around the walls of the building as well.

Half an hour later both the publicist and Marvin finally arrived, entering through the back entrance of the building, which looked more like a staff car park than anything else. I was introduced to Marvin who was wearing dark-rimmed glasses, a blue shirt and Khaki trousers. Due to everything now running slightly behind schedule, I was quickly ushered into the spacious boardroom where Hank and I took our seats for the interview.

He told me he'd been doing promo all day and that after our interview he was scheduled to fly out to Sydney on his next stop on the promo trail for his new album *Guitar Man*. As I took my seat, I told Hank what an honour it was to finally meet him and that how when I was fifteen I learned a lot of guitar playing from *20 Golden Greats*. He was genuinely very pleased to hear that, and began sharing with me the story about a teacher friend he knew and how he used the album to learn guitar and then used it to teach his students as well. "We all start off by copying someone we really admire but, if we've got any creative bone in our body, we will have to move on. We will have to develop our own music and that is what it should be about". Words of wisdom indeed!

Hank was very talkative and enjoyed telling his stories in-depth. A few minutes into our conversation, I turned on my Dictaphone and began our interview proper. The first few questions took around ten minutes to answer as Marvin really went in-depth. I enjoyed hearing his many stories particularly of those of the recording sessions at Abbey Road. Fascinating as well was his explanation of how 'Apache' took seven takes to record, though he stressed that a take back then wasn't necessarily one complete run through. A take would also include any false starts. He revealed that the recording of their first album, *The Shadows* (1961) was done in four three-hour recording sessions. Things were done quickly in the studio in those days. Usually what was expected were three finished tracks done in a three hour session and that's recorded and mixed! And the first time he ever double-tracked his guitars was on the track 'Foot Tapper' (1962).

I asked him also about how he came to be first guitarist in England to play the now famous Fender Stratocaster with which he became synonymous. "At that time you couldn't get new US instruments in the UK due to the trade embargo which had been in existence since the war. Cliff offered to buy me a really good guitar and we decided it had to be a Fender as Buddy Holly used one. So we got a Fender brochure over to the UK and I saw this beautiful photograph of a red Stratocaster that had a bird's eye maple neck, gold plated hardware and a tremolo arm, so we ordered the guitar. I started using that Fender Strat from Cliff's second album in 1959 and the Shadows' single at the time, a vocal track called 'Saturday Dance' which was the last track we did before we went in to record 'Apache'."

Around twenty minutes later the publicist quietly walked into the room and signalled to wrap up the interview but I wasn't done yet as Marvin was in the middle of answering a question, so I kept going for a couple more questions before the publicist gave me the eye! I mentioned to Marvin that I had a couple more questions and would he mind, even though our time was up, if he could answer them for me? He replied, "Of course, please do" so I quickly asked the questions which he proceeded to answer for me. In the end I got about a twenty-five minute in-depth interview which was great even though I still had more questions I could have asked but it was time for him to go. I asked him if he could sign some CD covers for me and he happily obliged.

As I was preparing to leave, he asked me about my band, "Obviously, you play in a band?"

"Yes I do" I replied. Before continuing, "I play covers of '70s and '80s classics" At the time I was playing in a covers band called Double Vision. He showed real interest and talked with me some more. I told him that I had an acoustic duo as well that played rock and pop tracks.

I got the impression that if time permitted, we could have talked all day and knowing that I was a musician interested him. As I walked out I noticed another journalist waiting for his turn to interview him.

I found Marvin very passionate about his music, especially when it came to guitars. He was always smiling and punctuated his answers with a delightful sense of humour. Hank was sixty-five at the time, yet although his hair was tinged with grey, he looked remarkably younger than that. It was such an honour to meet him. A few years later I got the chance to talk to Marvin again, albeit via a phone interview. Surprisingly he actually remembered me. Again he was as passionate and openly welcoming as he was that day back in 2007, and it was a pleasure yet again.

A man who had a similar kind of wit and openness to Mr Marvin was legendary Doors keyboardist Ray Manzarek, who I met one afternoon in 2007. Manzarek, who co-founded The Doors with Jim Morrison in 1965, was in town on a promo tour and the interview took place at stylishly upmarket Como Hotel in South Yarra. The promo was centred on the recently released set of The Doors reissues that were celebrating forty years since the band's debut album *The Doors* in 1967. It was a double celebration of sorts for Manzarek as it coincided with forty years of marriage to his wife Dorothy Fujikawa.

It was a Wednesday and the mid-week bustle of South Yarra was in full swing by the time I arrived at The Como adjoins the television studios of the TEN Network. As I waited in the hotel's lobby, I began a conversation with The Doors' Australian record label rep from Warner Music. My scheduled interview time was running about ten minutes late as Manzarek wanted to change into another set of clothes and grab a drink as he was having quite an intense day doing media and had been since 9 that morning. He still had another handful of interviews to do after mine, which meant his day would end at 7. The next day he was due to fly to Japan and he had only arrived a couple days earlier in Sydney. These kinds of promo tours are very much like that; full on schedules with as much crammed in as possible to utilize the artist's time. It can get quite exhausting at times for the artist in question.

Finally the time had come to make my way to the third floor for my interview, upon arrival at his room I again waited for a few more minutes as security, in the form of Manzarek's brother, informed us that Ray would just be a minute.

Soon after, we were ushered into his luxurious suite. As I entered, Manzarek was making himself a cup of tea. Dressed in a black-greyish zip-up jumper, black shirt, trousers and matching shoes, he was surprisingly tall with spikey short cropped greying hair that was tinged with shades of black and wearing glasses.

I greeted Manzarek with a simple 'hello' and he replied quickly observing some CD covers I had brought along with me, 'hello, you have things to sign?' So he reached for a marker pen as he made his way towards me. Manzarek's manager was sat in the dining area and after being introduced to him I sat down in front of the lounge table next to him, where he would quietly observe the interview proceedings whilst reading a magazine. Manzarek took a seat opposite us while the record label rep quietly paced the room. His "security guard" brother sat in the corner of the room. The Melbourne sun shone through the master bedroom's window, sending a glorious ray of sunshine throughout the room.

At the time Manzarek was 68 and looked in very good health. I found him very talkative and extremely passionate about The Doors music and served up many anecdotes along the way. He was very articulate, highly intelligent and extremely witty. On several occasions the room was filled with laughter. He was very animated in his demeanour and when he replied to your questions, he looked you straight in the eye. During our conversation he told me that the band, now known as Riders On The Storm, were planning to tour Australia in early 2008 and mentioned the band's new singer as ex-Fuel vocalist Brett Scallions. Scallions was taking over the lead vocalist spot after previous front-man Ian Astbury had returned to his own band The Cult. Astbury had joined Manzarek and Doors guitarist Robby Krieger after they reunited in 2001 under the moniker The Doors Of The 21st Century.

At one stage our conversation moved to the topic of the infamous Miami incident that occurred in 1969 where Jim Morrison allegedly exposed himself. Ray stated that because of what happened on that night, which was the first of that tour's dates, the tour ended as soon as it began! He recalled Morrison telling the audience on the night, "You've come to see something tonight, haven't you? You want to see my cock, don't you?"

Ray added with tongue firmly planted in his cheek that, "Well, I'm sure ladies would have loved to see a cock through those leather pants of his, but for me, I prefer nice tits and a round ass" this brought laughter to all of us in the room. He also painted a picture of the pain and boredom The Doors drummer John Densmore felt in the studio, when producer Paul A. Rothchild would spend days on end trying just to get his drum sound. He also talked about his keyboard playing particularly about his style of playing bass with his left hand.

I was eager to ask him whether over the years the cult of Jim Morrison had overshadowed much of the other band member's contribution to The Doors. He paused for a moment and then replied, "If it does, who cares? And if it does, I guess you're not really a music fan, you're sort of a personality fan, a fan of the leather pants and the penis. At the end of the day, as long they enjoy the music. Whatever it takes to get them into the music, be an intellectual, be a poet, be a young person coming up and discovering The Doors for the first time or whether it'll be guys or girls so inclined to be in love with Jim Morrison's bulge, as long as they get into the music at some point or another. That's the main thing. And get into Jim's poetry. Jim always said, 'Just listen to the words man, Just listen to the words'".

When asked how he kept The Doors songs sounding fresh today when performing them, he replied "I improvise!" He was happy to talk about The Doors legacy and anything to do with it and considering the amount of times over the years he must have spoken about it, he genuinely expressed loads of enthusiasm during my interview. The Doors legacy meant a lot to him. And then just as I was getting comfortable with the interview, it was time to wrap it all up. As I wished him well for the rest of his stay, he kindly told me how much he enjoyed our interview, which gave me much joy. Sadly, Ray passed away in 2013 but the music he made continues to live on.

When it comes to legends, few bands deserve the title more than British four-piece Queen. With such an iconic front man in the form of Freddie Mercury, the band's signature song 'Bohemian Rhapsody' has grown in stature and influence since its 1975 release. And for Queen guitarist Brian May, his unique style has influenced many guitarists including myself. If you listen to my song 'Louder Than Words' you'll hear a bit of that Queen guitar influence permeating my song.

Australia's love affair with Queen didn't get off on the right foot. When the band first visited these shores in early 1974 to perform at the Sunbury music festival, one of Australia first major festivals that took its inspiration from festivals such as Woodstock, they were virtually unknown and were booed and heckled amidst of calls for them to 'go back to Pommy land'. It also didn't help their cause being the only international act on an all-Australian bill and the fact that the Englishmen also brought along their own lighting rig and crew. The less than stellar response from the audience prompted Queen's lead singer Freddie Mercury to state to all those present on that day that, "when we come back to Australia, Queen will be the biggest band in the world!". Mercury's words proved prophetic as two years later when the band did return for their second visit, in the wake of the huge commercial and charting success of 'Bohemian Rhapsody', they were indeed one of the hottest acts on the scene.

So it was such an honour when I got to finally meet and interview Brian May back in March 2003 in Melbourne. At the time Brian, along with Queen drummer Roger Taylor, were in Australia preparing the launch of the Australian version of their *We Will Rock You* musical.

Melbourne would become the first time that the smash-hit Queen musical would be staged outside of London's West End. While both May and Taylor were in town, they also spent time scouring local talent for the 36-member cast and nine-piece band for the show. At the time of their visit more than 1,000 Australians had auditioned for the show which was to have its Australian première later that year in Melbourne at the prestigious Regent Theatre on August 7.

Media had been invited to the press conference that

was being held by May, Taylor and the musical's writer Ben Elton on a Thursday morning at a rehearsal studio above South Yarra's upmarket Chapel Street. It was a hectic schedule for both Brian and Roger on the day, with countless journalists wanting to have their time with them for a chat.

As each journalist entered the room, spread out on one of the tables set up near the entrance were boxes of Queen's 'Greatest Hits' CDs that were offered freely to the media present. I managed to secure a copy myself and later got Brian to sign the CD.

After the press conference was over, journalists gathered around each Queen member waiting for their turn for an interview. The big haired May graciously offered me some interview time after I had mentioned to him that the subject matter I would focus on was about guitar and his guitar playing.

Stepping aside to a quiet corner of the room, Brian and I began our chat. We discussed his guitar playing career with Queen and beyond. Topics covered included his then planned collaboration with Dave Stewart from The Eurythmics, Freddie Mercury's legacy and his four favourite guitar albums, which he told me were: *Bluesbreakers with Eric Clapton* (1966), Jimi Hendrix's *Axis: Bold As Love* (1967), Van Halen's self-titled debut, *Van Halen* (1978) and Jeff Beck's *Guitar Shop* (1989), particularly the track 'Where Were You' on that album which he stated to me, "... is the single most beautiful piece of guitar music ever recorded."

Regarding his Star Fleet Project in 1983 which resulted in a mini-album release, he said, "It was a wonderful experience, very loose. We didn't go in with the idea of making the album. We went with the idea of just having fun and putting it to tape. Making that album was one of the most influential things on me, as suddenly it made me realize there was a world outside [Queen]. I felt I needed to get out and interact again and playing with him [Eddie Van Halen] was brilliant".

I found him quietly spoken, generous, humble and very welcoming. He spoke with so much heart felt emotion when it came to Freddie Mercury, you could tell he truly missed him. He loved talking about guitars and music so much that we could have chatted for hours. Yet after about fifteen minutes Brian had to move onto the next journalist such was the interest in talking to him.

A decade later in August 2014 Brian sent me an email to personally invite my wife Liz and I to the Queen + Adam Lambert show at Rod Laver Arena in Melbourne as the band were touring Australia at the time. It was the first Queen tour of Australia since April 1985 when they were touring in support of their critically acclaimed *The Works* album. This time they were performing two shows while in Melbourne. The invite was for their second show and it included an opportunity to meet Brian again back stage after the show for a catch up. I was chuffed that Brian had remembered me from our initial interview back in 2003.

The invite afforded us good seats located close to the very front of the stage, where we watched the whole glorious show that featured a hits filled set. Adam Lambert had some big shoes to fill, but he performed magnificently and though he was no copy of Freddie Mercury, he brought his own personality and energy to the show. He certainly fitted perfectly into Mercury's shoes and I'm sure Freddie would have been proud.

After the show we were instructed to wait at a designated area before we were finally escorted backstage to the band's dressing room. Brian didn't look like he'd aged much in the years since I'd seen him although his hair had now gone white. He had changed out of his stage clothes and was now sporting, and quite proudly, a black 'I Love Melbourne' tee-shirt. This time it was more of a relaxed setting as some of the band's family and close friends were also in attendance and soaking up the atmosphere backstage. There was conversation and drinks aplenty amongst those present. Brian, who has a doctorate in astrophysics, and I chatted for a while with both my wife and I and he also generously offered me a bit of a play of his iconic signature Red Special guitar, nicknamed 'The Fireplace' due to the fact it was originally constructed by May and his father from pieces of wood from an old Victorian era fireplace, which made for a very memorable experience. It's not every day one gets to play Brian May's guitar!

When news of the passing of producer Sir George Martin filtered through in March 2016 the world lost not only a music legend but a *bona fide* member of the rock echelon. Martin – who was knighted in 1996 - together with The Beatles forever changed the course of music history and Sir George's importance in The Beatles story cannot be understated. Martin has been called 'The Fifth Beatle' since he was their producer during the entire existence of the band and also because he was the man solely responsible for signing them to a recording contract in 1962. When The Beatles first appeared on the Ed Sullivan Show on February 9th 1964 on American television, it forever changed the course of music history. Almost every post World War Two born guitarist or artist I've interviewed over the years cited that Beatles TV appearance as altering their life forever and the only reason why they pursued music as a lifestyle and career choice. Sir George also holds the record of the most number 1 records (30) in the UK by a producer.

In October 2002, I was hand-picked by Sir George to interview him. I was one of a privileged few as I had been informed that Sir George had knocked back about 60 other interview requests, so to be given the opportunity to interview a man of his stature was quite an honour and one of the highlights of my music journalism career.

Ironically around the same time I had also been offered an interview with Lifehouse, an American band that were at that time breaking through into the mainstream with their song 'Hanging By A Moment'. Their interview was scheduled to happen on the same day and time! For a few days, I was 'umming and ahhing' but eventually I declined the Lifehouse interview, and thankfully I made the right decision otherwise I would have passed on one of the biggest interviews of my career, and would have regretted it. It is not every day that one gets the chance to interview and meet someone that was a giant of the music industry and rock royalty of the highest order.

At the time of my interview Sir George was in Australia to launch and promote his lavishly illustrated 330-page autobiography *Playback* which was being issued by Genesis Publications, a publishing company that specialized in hand-signed limited editions. 2000 copies, each signed by Sir George, were issued by the publisher, and each going for a price of around $AUD900 per copy. The official launch of the book would occur the following week in Sydney.

Prior to the interview I had asked myself, 'what question would you ask someone like Sir George who probably has been asked every question possible when it came to The Beatles?' I mulled over this for quite a while, but I was determined to ask him questions that were different, and which would garner different types of answers than usual. So I spent quite a number of weeks, researching heavily and eventually I put together some really unique questions. On the morning of the interview, I woke up very early as I wanted to make sure I was well prepared and ready to go, leaving nothing to chance. George was staying at the Hotel Windsor which has the unofficial name of the Duchess of Spring Street - the hotel has played host to many international heads of government, royalty, celebrities, Hollywood stars and sporting legends over the years.

Sir George and his wife Lady Judy Martin greeted me at their suite located on one of the upper floors of the hotel and invited me in. Standing tall – over six feet - and silver haired, he looked fantastic for his age considering he was seventy-six by then. We took our seats and as Sir George sipped on a cup of tea, I hoped I'd found a few questions he'd never been asked! Sir George answered my questions in-depth and passionately, and shared many stories from his life and production career that were both fascinating and captivating. Over the course of half an hour he discussed various topics and insights into his production approach as well as working with The Beatles, how the recording process with The Beatles evolved over time (the first Beatles album took ten hours to complete while Sgt. Pepper took over 700 hours) and his strained relationship with John Lennon. Being a guitar player myself I was curious to ask him who his favourite guitar player was. To which he answered:

"Jeff Beck is probably our greatest rock guitar player ever! He uses his guitar as a voice and makes it sing. He actually does his performance like Mick Jagger does, but through his instrument. He's a hell of a talent. I've only made two albums with him though [*Blow By Blow* (1975),

Wired (1976)]. We've always promised each other that we would make another one, but we never did, but he did do a track for me on my last album *In My Life* [1998] where he did 'A Day In A Life'".

With the music industry in a state of flux at the time of the interview, I asked him for his views on the matter. "It's heading towards perdition at the moment. There's a tremendous amount of problems besetting the record business at the moment. One thing I think is that the audience has changed an awful lot, it's no longer the one we used to have ten or twenty years ago. The audience now is indoctrinated by computer screens and by television screens and by even hand held screens in your little texting machines. Everything is visual and kids now listen with their eyes not with their ears anymore. So, the artists they pick are those that are good looking chicks or guys who move well. It doesn't matter about the voice or song, but as long as they look good".

And when I asked him how he approached the task of being a producer, he stated, "The way I produce is I like to lead, I like to coax people along and say 'this is the way to do it and you're going to have fun with it'. Then they have fun and they sparkle and then let themselves go and totally forget that there's a microphone in front of them and a big screen. So, they then start performing".

We could have chatted for hours, but time was flying by so quickly that all too quickly it was time to conclude the interview. As I always did during my meetings I asked for a photo with him, and he kindly obliged and then I asked him what his plans were for the next few days. He smiled and said that he was planning to take the next few days off from all media obligations in order to travel into the country and take in the scenery and just do some relaxing as well, before he had to continue on his way to the launch up in Sydney.

Status Quo are true rock 'n' roll legends, still rocking all over the world fifty plus years on with worldwide record sales that total in excess of 100 million. And they're also one of the bands that over the years, especially during their golden period throughout the 1970s and 1980s, were notorious for their hard partying, drug taking and hedonistic over indulgence. I first met and interviewed Quo vocalist and lead guitarist Francis Rossi and rhythm guitarist Rick Parfitt while the band were in Melbourne during April 2003 as part of their *Heavy Traffic* Australian Tour 2003.

The interview took place at the rather chic Stamford Plaza Melbourne Hotel the day before their first Melbourne show, which was happening at the Mercury Lounge - now defunct - located inside Crown Casino. It was also the first show of their Australian tour. After doing a lap around the country, they'd return to Melbourne two weeks later to perform their final show of the tour at the Palais Theatre in St Kilda. The band later gave me passes to both shows, and I reviewed one of the shows for *Classic Rock Magazine* in the UK.

When I arrived for the interview I noticed Rick sitting in the next room doing an interview with a newspaper journalist. Soon after Rick's interview got wrapped up and the journalist left, so the publicist introduced me to. Rick who was well-dressed and looked a picture of good health. Sporting a silver watch and with a golden mane and dark sunglasses, he looked every bit the rock star. I was informed Francis was on his way up so we decided to start the interview without him. A few questions in Francis finally surfaced and joined us. The band's manager and publicist sat opposite us around the table and watched proceedings unfold. Both answered my questions with brutal honesty and punctuated each answer with hilarity especially Francis who had a wicked English humour, though his answers to my questions tended to a lot shorter than Rick's.

Both came across as very down to earth people; intelligent, passionate and oozed with a sense of warmth and joy that was highly infectious. They did not shy away from answering questions about their drug addled days in the 1970s - or what they could remember from it - or the split with former band members.

Rick also seemed to be a lot more open to my questions and his answers were in-depth even though remembering things proved somewhat of a problem for him especially when it came to topics revolving around the 'Whatever You Want' (1979) period. "We were doing far too much coke then so with that whole period, I can't remember!".

Francis chimed in saying that he still had a hole in his nose where the septum used to be, the result of his heavy drug intake from those years. However when it came to the subject of guitars, they happily went into great detail about it all. They also told me they were in the middle of writing an autobiography. That book, *Status Quo: XS All Areas*, would eventually be released a year later, in late 2004. The interview was very enjoyable and loads of fun due to Francis' comical banter.

After the interview was over they kindly signed my CD and I got a photo with both and then their manager informed them that they had a fifteen minute break before their next interview. Francis left the room and I asked Rick for a guitar pick. Rick told me he didn't have one on him, but asked me to wait while he went back to his hotel room to get one for me and he returned a few minutes later with one for me! I thanked him and bid him goodbye left with the publicist who told me "that's the best interview I've ever sat in on," which brought a smile to my face.

The next night my wife Liz and I made our way to The Mercury Lounge in the Casino precinct where the band was playing their first Australian show of the current tour. The band hit the stage at around 9.30pm and played a blistering set that encompassed old and new material off their most recent album *Heavy Traffic*. The stage set was very much reminiscent of the album's cover art. They finished their set with a medley of rocking tracks. We returned again a couple weeks later at the band's invitation to their final Melbourne show. The night was a similar affair as their Mercury Lounge show two weeks earlier though on this night they added a few other songs that allowed more space for Francis to indulge in guitar solos. That evening's set was even better than the first, obviously all the shows since then had made the band tighter and more polished. All in all, that night's show was just as brilliant.

I next saw the band three years later when they toured Australia again as part of a co-headlining bill with Deep Purple under the moniker of the *Double Trouble* tour. Though both bands shared the same age demographic, in my opinion they were musically poles apart. I wrote the following review of the show for a magazine: "The Palais Theatre proved the perfect setting for both playing amidst the lavish theatre surrounds and seated facilities of the historic theatre. The 2,500 plus seater was filled to the brim as Quo hit the stage just after 8.00pm. Firing off with one of Quo's early classics in the form of 'Caroline', Status Quo held the crowd in their hands for their entire performance.

With their set cut back to 70 minutes to fit the frame work of the double bill schedules, they bulldozed their way through their set pulling out all the stops with their sweaty boogie rock. Serving up a slice of some of their best offerings they came thick and fast: 'The Oriental', 'All Stand Up', 'Whatever You Want', 'Down, Down', 'Rain', '4500' and closer 'Rockin' All Over The World', all testified to Quo's majestic power. As soon as it began, it seemed it was over. And the crowd were wanting more. It was here that things turned, unfortunately, against Deep Purple.

"With a grey-haired and barefooted Ian Gillian at the helm, Deep Purple kicked off an uninspiring set, that was mostly comprised of album tracks and less familiar numbers. The ordering of the set list did them no favours. Suddenly people started to leave. In fact after putting up with a handful of tracks myself, the boredom was so great, I too up and left. I felt sorry for the Purple though as the last time I saw them in 2004 they were on fire and unstoppable, but tonight the fire was totally non-existent. Personally, I feel no band can compete with the sheer power of the mighty Quo. It was a match not made in heaven. In the end Quo stole the show underscoring why their appeal continues to endure with fans after 40 years in the business. And who knows, maybe Purple learned a thing or two tonight. Let's hope Purple aspire to redeem themselves next time round. But tonight, Quo were King and definitely rocked all over the world..."

I must admit, whether you like them or not, Quo's brand of boogie rock always puts a smile on concert goers and each gig is just as memorable as the last. Meeting Francis and Rick left me with wonderful lasting impressions and memories. In 2010, both were also appointed to The Most Excellent Order Of The British Empire. The world sadly lost Rick in December 2016 but his spirit continues to live on through Quo's music.

15 - SHANG-A-LANG

Tartan sensations Bay City Rollers were the first *bona fide* boy band in the 1970s with their easily digestible pop tunes that caused hysteria wherever they went. Having sold over 100 million albums they were one of the biggest selling acts of the decade. Led by baby-faced poster boy Les McKeown, who was only eighteen when he joined the group in 1974, the group also included Eric Faulkner and Stuart 'Woody' Wood both on guitar, Alan Longmuir on bass and his brother Derek on drums and enjoyed a remarkable few years of worldwide popularity with a run of Top 10 hits that included two UK number ones in 1975 with 'Bye, Bye, Baby' (which hit #1 also in Australia) and 'Give A Little Love' (which peaked at #2 on the Australian charts) and a US number 1 with 'Saturday Night' in 1976 and embarked on their first Australian tour at the tail end of 1975. McKeown acrimoniously left the band for a solo career in 1978 that was met with huge success in Japan, by which time the band's popularity had waned. In the aftermath The Bay City Rollers renamed themselves The Rollers and soldiered on with South African singer Duncan Faure for another three albums which were largely overlooked.

The band always seemed to be surrounded by drama wherever they went, especially in Australia. During one of the band's reunion tours of the country in the mid–1980s, a bomb scare at one of their concerts saw the audience evacuated and on another occasion guitarist Eric Faulkner walked out on the band at the tour's completion.

Throughout the 1990s and 2000s the band spent considerable time in legal wrangling over owed royalties and name ownership and by this point the group had splintered into different versions with one band called The New Rollers led by Eric Faulkner and another under the original name of Bay City Rollers led by Stuart Wood. Beginning in the 2000s McKeown also led a new version of the band but under The Bay City Rollers moniker although he was the sole original member in the line-up.

It was with this line-up comprised of McKeown along with Phil Hendriks on guitar, Scott McGowan on keys and guitar, Dan Guest on drums and Si Roller on bass that toured Australia in 2017 and to which I was offered and accepted the support slot, opening for the band at their two sold-out shows in Melbourne.

I was too young to have witnessed the band live in concert in 1975 but I was a fan and had their records. At the time it wasn't cool to admit being a fan among the male fraternity at my school, but I never cared as I thought the band's hugely catchy pop tunes were great. To me it was pop music at its best. I even wore the tartan socks that were part of the band's merchandising. Many derided the band back then have since come clean and admitted their love for the band and music. Over the years everyone from The Ramones, who credit 'Saturday Night' for inspiring their very own classic 'Blitzkrieg Bop', to the late Malcolm McLaren who stated that Sex Pistols were modelled on Bay City Rollers and they were even name checked by Nirvana's Kurt Cobain.

My first experience of the band live was when McKeown last toured Australia in 2007 as part of the second *Countdown Spectacular* Tour, a packaged nostalgia tour that did the rounds of the country and featured classic Australian and international acts from the 1970s and 1980s that were part of the Australian music television programme *Countdown*, Australia's very own take on the UK's *Top Of The Pops*. The 2017 tour was billed as *The Greatest Hits* tour. When the tour was announced ticket sales went through the roof and more shows were added due to demand. The band ended up performing 16 shows around the country, most of which were sold-out. It was incredible that forty years after their heyday the band was still able to pull in the crowds and sell-out shows.

Once I was confirmed for the support slots in May 2017 I waited with excitement for the first of my two shows with the band on June 30 at Shoppingtown Hotel, a suburban hotel cum live music venue in Doncaster, about a thirty-minute drive east of Melbourne. Arriving around mid-afternoon a handful of tartan clad fans were already loitering around the venues back entrance and car park. Mainly female and middle aged, they stood firm with cameras in hand hoping to capture a minute with their idols. As my wife and I made our way to the load-in area, Phil Hendriks and Si Roller appeared outside. Si was on his phone taking a call while Hendriks took a few moments out to have a cigarette as the fans gathered around him and began chatting. He put out his cigarette and quickly returned inside while Si continued with his call. I made my way over to him and introduced myself telling him I was the support act and he led us into the venue. A couple of fans, seeing us, quickly tried to join us, as if they were part of our entourage so they could sneak their way into the venue!

Inside the place was abuzz with activity, as crew continued setting up the stage and sound equipment. The band members were preparing to sound check without

Les. Quite a large room, it could house around 1,000 people standing room only, and I was informed the show was a sell-out and had been for weeks. The call then went out that sound check was about to get underway. They began by running through 'Rock 'n' Roll Love Letter' and once the sound was tweaked further they kicked into a medley of classic songs that paid tribute to friends and bands of theirs, particularly of Les, that he'd known during the course of Bay City Rollers' career. The medley kicked off with 'Bohemian Rhapsody' (Queen) and segued into '20th Century Boy' (T-Rex), then 'Tiger Feet' (MUD), and 'My Coo Ca Choo' (Alvin Stardust) then 'Rebel, Rebel' (Bowie) and 'Blockbuster' (The Sweet) before returning and finishing with another bout of 'Bohemian Rhapsody'. The band was tight and sounded superb and happy with it all, they declared the sound check done.

I was instructed to set up for my sound check and since my set up was simple, just an acoustic guitar, some pedals and vocals, I took no longer than fifteen minutes with my sound check. At 5:30pm Les finally surfaced – dressed casually in blue jeans and a dark coloured coat, he walked onstage and had a look around and checked on things. When he finished, I made my way over and introduced myself. We greeted each other and he warmly welcomed me. First thing he said to me in his thick Scottish accent was, "I checked you out on You Tube, and I really like your music". I had been informed Les had personally selected the artists who would be his band's support.

Both Liz and I were invited to share the band's dressing room and as we made our way there, Si Roller was in the corner busy ironing his stage clothes. A table with bottles of water, beer, spirits and snacks was laid out on one side of the room. Not long after we had all settled in, the venue's manager walked in and instructed us that dinner was about to be served for the band in an adjoining room which had been cordoned off so they could dine in private. He escorted all of us through the side passage way and into the room and asked us to take our seats.

We took our seats around a large table with Les sat to my right and Dan Guest on my left. Liz took her seat on Dan's other side and next to Phil Hendricks. Les enjoyed a steak and veggie dish but I noticed he didn't eat much of it, the reason he gave was being worried about getting food poisoning again! He mentioned that on their flight to Australia at their first stop over in Dubai he had suffered food poisoning and had to be escorted off the plane in a wheelchair until a doctor cleared him to travel onward. Then upon arrival at Sydney, he got another bout of food poisoning. Dan told Liz and I that he had just got married and went on his honeymoon but soon after he was off on tour again.

After dinner we made our way back to the green room. We continued chatting and having some drinks while waiting for the doors to open and the show to begin. The fans were already starting to line-up outside and a long line was quickly forming readying themselves for the doors to finally open. Before the doors opened fans who had purchased the special VIP meet 'n' greet packages were allowed entry first and taken to a room set up for that purpose. Les changed into his tartan outfit chatting to us, he casually took off his pants and continued talking – my wife didn't know which way to look! After he had put on his full tartan outfit, Les went off to meet his fans. He chatted to every single one, signed all their items and happily posed with them for photos and then hugged them each goodbye.

After about half an hour he returned and changed again, this time swapping his tartan shirt for a different tartan shirt which he'd wear on stage. He continued chatting and sharing stories from his life and career. I asked how he managed the jet lag, and he said, 'I'm still feeling it and have been having trouble trying to get my sleep cycle back". He added that he got so frustrated on his first night in Sydney that he had to pull out the power cord from the hotel's room fridge as the the noise was disturbing his sleep. The jet lag was clearly kicking in with both Scott and Dan who decided to lie across their couches to catch up for a quick nap before show time.

Finally the doors opened and the fans, mostly female, filtered through into the venue. The merchandise desk did brisk business selling Les's recently self-released solo album *The Lost Songs* containing songs he had written some of which dated back forty years and were intended for Bay City Rollers albums but were never used. His initial plan was to release it as an actual Bay City Rollers album and while the other former members seemed to be in favour, Stuart Wood nixed the idea altogether so Les was left with issuing it as a solo album. The CD and all the other Bay City Rollers merchandise would eventually sell out half way through the Australian tour.

My support slot was 30 minutes long while the band's show was around 80 minutes. With the crowd now increasing in size and the room filling up quickly, I got given a five minute show time warning, grabbed my guitar and prepared to stand by the stage until I was given the green light. As I took a peek behind stage curtain, the room was bursting at capacity with tartan clad females who were visibly getting excited for their musical heroes as the hour wore on. It was definitely the biggest audience I'd ever played to. I hit the stage to rapturous applause. As I plugged into the PA system, I heard a couple fans standing in front of the stage call my name in unison. The energy and excitement from the audience fed into my performance and I pulled out all the stops to put on my best show. As I wandered from side to side on the stage, I encouraged the audience to clap along and at times as I neared the front of the stage, tartan scarves were felt near my ankles as they flicked from side to side. Cameras were flashing away during the set and my songs were well received with much applause after each. As I played my final song and end of my set, I left the stage to the crowd yelling 'encore'!

As I returned to the dressing room, the guys congratulated me. They'd all changed into their stage clothes now and with show time getting nearer, we left them to it. As the lights dimmed the band hit the stage and kicked off their show with 'Summerlove Sensation' as the fans went into a frenzied state of excitement. The band performed a brilliant set of hits with only one new song 'Beautiful' off *The Lost Songs* album. They closed their set with their classic 'Bye, Bye Baby' and the audience sang along hoisting up their scarves.

After the gig I headed backstage to say my goodbyes to them all and wished them all the best for the rest of the shows and that I'd look forward to seeing them again in two weeks' time for their next Melbourne show.

After traversing the country, the band returned for their second sold-out Melbourne show two weeks later. This time they were playing the luxurious confines of Palms On Crown, located on the third floor of the Crown Casino at Southbank. The venue housed a cabaret-styled concert seat layout that has areas raising upwards every few sections with booths positioned around the room's perimeter.

I arrived mid-afternoon and was allocated a nice large dressing room all to myself with all the creature comforts available that included a bathroom, a couch, table and chairs, and lighted mirrors. A stark contrast to the dressing room I'd shared with the band at the last show. The band were also allocated their own rooms, Les's in particular was quite large and very deserving for the star of the show while the others shared. Les's room was off limits for the night, with his door shut so he could have some peace and quiet prior to the show. The tour manager was given his own room, where he set up his lap top and continued with the business at hand. The atmosphere backstage was very peaceful and relaxing. A well-stocked fridge sat in the corridor where band and crew could freely snag a drink or sandwiches and tea and coffee making facilities were freely available too.

When Les and the rest of the band arrived at the venue they headed to their allocated rooms. Les told me he didn't have far to go to return to his hotel as he was staying in the same building on one of the Casino's top floors. This time Les and the rest of the band gathered on the stage and prepared themselves for sound check. They spent the next hour and a half sound checking, running through several songs such as 'I Only Want To Be With You'. Les then did a cappella version of 'Give A Little Love' before the band joined him for the remainder of the songs. Around 6pm the band finally completed their sound check and I was directed to undertake my sound check which again took only about fifteen minutes running through some vocal and guitar line checks. By the time I'd finished, everyone had left the backstage area to go and have dinner. I ventured down to the food court where all the band members except Les, who was busy with the VIP meet 'n' greets in

174

the foyer, were looking at what was on offer for dinner. A large number of Roller fans had also filtered into the food court, and were eating dinner as they waited for doors to open. Doors finally opened after 7pm and fans started entering the venue and slowly took their seats. About half an hour later we all got a backstage message on the in-house PA informing us that "cast and crew, 15 minutes to show time". These were announced at five minute intervals until the 8pm show time.

Five minutes before show time I ventured out to the side of the stage with my guitar and waited patiently for the stage manager's direction to hit the stage. By this time the room had filled to capacity. Another sold-out show! Then the lights were dimmed, and given the all clear, I hit the stage which was huge in comparison to the Shoppingtown stage. I performed another set and the loud applause and cheers that greeted I walked off back to my dressing room were a buzz before I went backstage to relax and bask in the after show energy.

The Rollers hit the stage half an hour later to deafening applause and cheers. The evening's set had a different energy as Les seemed to get more of the crowd participation happening, even getting them to come to the front of stage and putting the mic in front of them so they could sing some of the words. He was also a lot more animated and as he kept moving across stage, reaching out to the fans, touching them one by one, as they came up to him while singing.

What an artist enjoys hearing is the feedback that fans sometimes offer up at shows. One Roller fan told me she loved my voice, while another complimented me by saying, "you were different but in a very good and enjoyable way". After two nights with Bay City Rollers, there definitely was an upswing in numbers of newly-converted Rollers fans becoming Joe Matera fans!

Backstage after the show everyone began preparations to return to their hotel. I said goodbye to everyone and wished them well on their last two shows of the tour after which they would begin the long journey home. Les gave me one last warm hug and complimented me on my performance saying, "You did great work". Then, as the clock ticked towards midnight, we all left the venue. It'd been an exhausting few weeks and the band were now missing their families so were looking forward to finally seeing them again but it would be short lived as after a few weeks off they would regroup and do it all again... and on and on it goes for the life of a touring musician.

Les and the band returned for another successful jaunt around the country the following year. They were scheduled to return again in 2020 but due to the Covid pandemic, the tour was rescheduled to 2021. Sadly the tour ended up being scrapped altogether when McKeown passed away at his home on April 20, 2021.

16 - SEX, DRUGS & ROCK 'N' ROLL

Sex, drugs and rock 'n' roll have been bedfellows since even before the counter-culture scene of the 1960s but it was the exploits of rock bands in the ensuing decades from the likes of The Rolling Stones, Led Zeppelin, Motley Crue and others which provided tabloid fodder and made the trio synonymous. The stories are legendary and well documented, for example the infamous Mud Shark incident in 1969 involving Led Zeppelin or KISS bassist Gene Simmons boastful claim to have bedded over 4,000 women or Motley Crue's 2001 tell all book, *The Dirt,* which detailed the band's outrageous debauchery, have all cemented the sex, drugs and rock 'n' roll association.

Ian Dury even wrote a song titled 'Sex and Drugs and Rock and Roll' in 1977 which immortalized the phrase into the vernacular. While many of the scandalous claims made by rock bands over the years have been found to have originated from publicists, a huge number have been genuine.

For KISS's fire-breathing bass player Gene Simmons, sex and rock 'n' roll went hand in hand. "Girls and lots of them certainly make my world go round" he told me in an interview in 2002. "The girls have always made every day above ground a good day. And when you think about it, it's the prime urge, the urge to merge! So any guy in a band who tells you that he's doing it because he's got music in his heart, well he's just lying. He's playing in a band because he wants to get laid! While the concerts are fantastic and fun, doing the encores back at the hotel are even more fun.

And the guy that tells you otherwise, is lying".

The late great Lemmy Kilmister was never one to ever shy away from any discussion of sex, drugs and rock 'n' roll during interviews. In an interview I did with him in early 2005, he told me about the time during the early days of Motörhead's existence in the 1970s when the band was on tour in Europe playing a set and a woman suddenly appeared out of nowhere onstage and proceeded to give him a blow job there and then. "That was amazing" he recalled. "The more I think about it now the more dream like it becomes. It was some college gig we did and I think she must have been on a dare or something. As afterwards she disappeared and I never saw her again".

For bands such as eighties American Glam-metal merchants Warrant who have been proud of their sex, drugs and rock 'n' roll mantra to the point they were happy to share their many exploits to anyone who listened. As the band's guitarist Joey Allen told me in 2004 when looking back at the band's height of popularity, "We used to have orgies going on at certain times. We were pretty racy when it came to the women and the amount of women we had and nothing was held back at all. Ever! In the early days when we were all single and having a good time, you can imagine what it was like. Anything you can imagine, I would ask you to just double it, because that was what it was like. We had this guy who would hand out passes to the girls to come back stage after the show and just party so things would go from there. Most of the time it pretty much 99% alcohol and 1% drugs whether some weed or blow. For example, during the *Cherry Pie* tour in 1991, we had this stage that was quite tall and we used to have, you know, 'parties' under the stage while there was a drum or guitar solo going on".

Tracii Guns, guitarist with fellow Glam-metallers L.A Guns, concurred with Allen when I spoke to him in 2005, "there was this time around '88 when we were still playing clubs and this beautiful girl was at the back of the tour bus and everybody was fuckin' her. Sometime later this guy came to the front of the bus asking if so and so was there. And we looked at this girl and knew it was her and she goes 'yeah he's my ex-boyfriend'. It turned out that the ex-boyfriend was really the boyfriend and was the same guy that had booked our gig, as well as being in the opening band and he had just paid us! And here we were, with everybody having just fucked his girlfriend. So we asked her to leave immediately."

Another band who epitomized rock 'n' roll's debauched lifestyle are American retro-rockers Hinder who first came onto the scene when they released their aptly title debut album *Extreme Behavior* in 2005. Hailing from Oklahoma City, the quintet formed in 2001 with their debut single 'Get Stoned' – an ode to partying being released in 2005, which further cemented their bad boy image. With the release of their biggest hit, 'Lips Of An Angel' the following year the band hit pay dirt and with it came the spoils of success. The band took their cue both musically and aesthetically from the 1980s Sunset Strip scene of the likes of Mötley Crüe and Guns N' Roses. In March 2007 the band toured down under for the first time as part of a promotional visit and I got to interview the band's lead guitarist Joe "Blower" Garvey.

Though the band's debut album had been out in the United States since September 2005, it had only just been released in Australia. So Hinder had finally arrived in Melbourne having been in the country for the past week, kicking off their inaugural Australian visit in Brisbane.

Melbourne would be their last port of call as they were
due to return home a couple days later. The promotional
visit saw the band scheduling their first Australian tour later
in that same year in October. Garvey told me they'd been
playing a lot of acoustic stuff on the promo tour and felt it
was not really indicative of what they are about as they just
wanted to rock out with the whole band live, both he and
the band were looking forward to the upcoming October
tour.

Garvey was in an upbeat mood and very cheery when I
met him and the first thing he said to me was, "Man, what
is it about Australian girls, they're so beautiful! There must
something in the water. I love this country and want to
stay here". Garvey, who earned his nickname of 'Blower'
for his predilection for blow jobs from groupies in front
of his band mates, oozed with an amiable spirit and a
refreshing honesty. He didn't shy away from opening up
about his debauched escapades and in fact revelled in them.
He admitted to being a huge fan of the TV reality series
Jackass, which figures given his character. Garvey would do
anything for a laugh, even going to the extreme lengths
of setting his own testicles on fire, something which to
an outsider revealed Garvey's tendency for sadomasochism
and self-mutilation.

He told me the band had been recording and
documenting all of their tour adventures, including their
inaugural Australian visit and said they had plans to release
different versions of it at some point in future which would
include an X-Rated version, a PG version and a *Jackass*
version. He confirmed that life on the road was one non-
stop party, and the band even had a Jägermeister machine
on their tour bus so that they could have ice cold shots on
tap 24/7.

Over the course of the interview he continued to recount many of his touring experiences and said the numerous pranks he'd had done which had left him with numerous scars but he just grinned when mentioning them. He certainly wasn't complaining, he took everything in stride and I sensed he enjoyed the whole shebang of the rock star lifestyle. Amid all the talk of his hijinks though, there was a moment where I glimpsed an inherent loneliness hidden away deep down. He was missing home and a sense of stability. Garvey said they'd been on the road almost non-stop for the past 21 months, and that he didn't really have a home at that moment. But one of his goals for the year he told me was that if a window of opportunity to take a short break from the treadmill of touring was possible, he'd go and purchase a house so that he could spend Christmas in his own place.

Our conversation then turned to the subject of the hit single 'Lips Of An Angel', and to what the song was really about. "It's about thinking of cheating but it actually never gets mentioned in the song," he pointed out that the closest it came to actually saying that specifically was in the line, "it's hard to be faithful". He added that 'Lips Of An Angel' was also a true story that happened to Austin Winkler (Hinder's lead singer), and that it was written one night during pre-production and only took 40 minutes to write. He explained that most of the material they'd written started off on acoustic guitars, and if the songs really grooved and sounded good on a stripped down acoustic, then they knew they had themselves a good song to work on with the electric guitars and the rest of the band. Joe was excited that Hinder were now the rock band to have sold the most ring tones in Australia which was around two million units at the time.

He told me several stories regarding Hinder's tour with Canadian post-grunge rockers Nickelback on their *All The Right Reasons* Tour the previous year. Garvey stated that Chad Kroeger, Nickelback's lead singer and guitarist, had a penchant for encouraging Garvey's pranks and debauchery. In fact on one occasion Kroeger offered the band the sum of $160 if anyone in the band was willing to have Garvey's testicles stapled to their butt. Hinder bassist Mike Rodden took up the challenge and won the money, leaving both with scars from the incident. On another occasion, while the band were in Kansas City on the last night of their tour Kroeger, knowing the band had an appetite for female strippers, decided instead to hire a group of male strippers to go on stage during Hinder's set which caused the audience to go into hysterics. "It wasn't funny for us" Garvey told me with a slight grin. "I wouldn't have minded if they were female!"

With my interview time with Garvey fast approaching an end, he kindly asked if I wanted the rest of the band to sign my CD album cover which I had brought along and he left and got all the members to sign the cover and then brought it back and introduced me to the rest of the band, except for Winkler who was running late and still on his way down from his hotel room. The band were scheduled to leave as soon as Winkler surfaced to head to Fox FM, a popular Melbourne rock radio station where they were scheduled to do a live interview and perform an acoustic rendition of 'Lips Of An Angel'.

Aside from the radio appearance, their schedule later that afternoon also included an in-store acoustic performance at a nearby record store. Garvey rushed back to his hotel room to fetch his guitar. Hinder rhythm guitarist Mark King had already come equipped with his acoustic and so while he and his fellow band mates waited for Winkler, he strummed through a few songs. He was soon joined by Garvey who returned with this guitar and together they both played through some stuff while waiting. I waited around enjoying the impromptu performance but with time against me I said my goodbyes and headed out. As I was just about to leave, Winkler finally surfaced and all quickly boarded their Tarago which was waiting outside the hotel's entrance to head to their radio engagement.

When the band finally returned in October for a full blown Australian tour I again got the opportunity to interview them. It had been just six months since I first met the testosterone charged rock outfit and wondered if in that period they had changed. This time around the band's press engagements were being conducted in the more modest surrounds of the Holiday Inn on Flinders. I waited for quite a while in the hotel's lobby which was abuzz with guests and visitors before the band finally arrived. Their publicist from Universal introduced me to the band's heavily tattooed bassist Mike Roden and rhythm guitarist Mark King who remembered me from the previous meeting. Both were dressed casually and sported wearing baseball caps.

We found a quiet area in the dining area away and were joined by Cody Hanson, the band's curly red-haired, bandanna wearing. Both Rodden and King ordered Vodkas as we took our seats. Since the band's debut album had come out in September 2005, the past two years had seen the band clock up over 700 shows which was a long time to be out on the road and which would be both physically and mentally hard going. King admitted that drinking lots of alcohol helped keep things on an even keel. I caught a glimpse of Winkler who quickly brushed through the lobby and made his way to the elevator where he disappeared out of sight. A Hinder crew member who was with Winkler came towards us and checked on things to make sure everything was cool.

Garvey later walked through the dining area. He had just returned from doing an interview himself. I called out, "Hey Joe, good to see you dude". He stopped, turned around and upon recognizing me shook my hand. With Garvey now standing beside us, both Rodden and King began telling me how Garvey had got his scrotum tattooed on their recent tour with Buckcherry and Papa Roach. Curiosity getting the better of me, I asked, "I got to see that".

"You shouldn't say that as Blower will show you", King answered.

"In fact, I have photos on my cell phone as proof!" Rodden said as he grabbed his phone and showed me the photos. In one of them, Blower stood naked holding up his penis where underneath on his scrotum you could clearly observe the word 'Heartbeat' tattooed across it.

"That must have been painful"

"What's amazing about it, is that Blower did it sober!" Rodden answered.

Both proceeded to share further debauched tales from the road; the sex, pranks, and further tales about the tour Hinder undertook with Massachusetts nu-metal outfit Staind.

"On the Staind tour we did, Blower pulled out his nuts onstage" Rodden continued, "and then we hosed them down with hair spray and lit his pubic hair on fire during the segment where Staind front man Aaron Lewis was playing an acoustic thing. And we went out and did that in front of him!"

"That wouldn't have gone down well with Lewis" I remarked.

"Yeah, but hey, we gave Aaron some pyro effects for his set!" Rodden laughed. "We are always doing stupid shit like that. Blower's also got an enormous talent for stretching his nut sack over many different things".

With talk of 'blow jobs' and 'scrotums' punctuating our interview, many hotel guests were beginning to turn heads as the conversation from the group increased in volume. A group of women sitting nearby overhearing the exchange began looking towards our direction. As the interview needed to wind up, I asked the pair one last question, which related to their plans for the evening. "We're going to some strip bars!" they exclaimed in unison. And with that, we said our goodbyes and the band along with the crew departed for the night's saucy adventures and left the hotel dining room in peace.

The band performed their show the next night at the Metro Nightclub, located inside the premises of a 108-year old theatre which had been home to live concerts since 1987, with the likes of everyone from James Brown to Jane's Addiction having strutted their stuff on stage. It would sadly close its doors in 2014. After the Australian tour, Hinder would finally bring to an end their two year world tour. They had planned to begin recording their second album which they were initially hoping to issue in early January 2008 but *Take It To The Limit* wouldn't see the light of day until November of that year.

After the band issued their fourth studio album, *Welcome to the Freakshow,* in December 2012, Austin Winkler entered rehab to deal with a drug addiction in early 2013 and would officially depart the band later that same year.

★

Scottish rockers Primal Scream were no strangers to substance abuse. In fact, the band took much pride in the fact and didn't shy away from the subject. Their electronica tinged rock has mostly been fuelled by the band's appetite for hard drugs as I found out when I met up with them in Melbourne in February 2009. The band was in town as part of the Australian leg of their *Welcome To Your Beautiful Future* Tour which was undertaken in support of their ninth studio album *Beautiful Future* which had been released a year earlier. It had been nine years since the band were last in the country.

I caught up with the band on the Monday afternoon after their Sunday night Melbourne show at Billboard, a mid-size live venue in the heart of Melbourne that has a capacity of around 1,000 people. It's a venue I have performed at myself when back in March 2018 I was the support act for Irish soul-ster Andrew Strong of *The Commitments* fame.

Primal Scream's post-punk beginnings had evolved over the years and eventually the band embraced the late-'80s acid-house sound and with it the party lifestyle. The interview was supposed to happen at the Hilton Hotel [where the band were staying] at 2pm but at lunch time I was notified that it had been rescheduled to 4pm. As I had already arrived in time for the scheduled 2pm meeting, the band's publicist invited me to drop by their offices in Carlton to hang around until interview time. Upon arrival, the publicist explained that the handful of interviews scheduled for the day were now under a cloud of uncertainty as the tour manager had just told informed the publicist, that all interviews might now be cancelled.

My interview had been confirmed with two members of the band – bassist Mani and guitarist Andrew Innes. In the end Mani never surfaced so Innes was confirmed to do the interview alone which was now rescheduled, yet again, to 5pm along with a change of location as well, to the Regency Bar inside The Marriot Hotel which lay conveniently down the road and within walking distance of the venue.

The publicist was mystified as to why the band wanted to do it at the new location rather than their hotel and it was clear that they were getting on her nerves. We eventually walked the distance from the record label offices to The Marriot, all the while with the publicist trying desperately to call the tour manager. Eventually Innes, keyboardist Martin Duffy (who we had no idea was going to join us until the last minute) and the band's youthful tour manager, who looked like he'd just graduated from university, finally met us in the hotel foyer. They all seemed to be on something as Innes told me the reason they chose the bar for the interview was because the last time they were in Melbourne nine years earlier, the bar man there had made them the best Daiquiri.

Hearing this, the publicist went off and ordered them some Daiquiris, though as it turned out they didn't like them, which they proceeded to tell the publicist, explaining that they were the way the original guy had made them. They spoke in thick Scottish accents and Innes and Duffy certainly looked and acted like two old men high on a cocktail of drugs. And both looked like they had a hard night and had just got out of bed there and then. Duffy looked like he had just come home after a day's work at the farm! Eventually the subject matter turned to drugs.

I mentioned that their breakthrough album *Screamadelica* felt drug-induced. "You're right about that album" Innes replied, "we were taking pills and it was an influence on that album. It has been different drugs for different albums though. Usually there would be one drug that would unify it though. But cocaine is the one that universally will ruin everything. We abandoned the 'Rocks' sessions because we were in such a drugged out state. I remember our record company guy Alan McGee phoning us up and saying, 'guys you're going to have a hit with 'Rocks'. And I'm on the phone going, I don't remember recording it. And he says, 'Well, I have the recording here in my hands!'"

Innes recalled another recording session in particular when drugs spiralled the band out of control. "There was this one time where we were recording the track 'Come Together' for *Screamadelica*, our drummer had come into the studio with this big bag of pills. We asked him what they were and he said that they were the pills that killed Keith Moon. And we went, 'if they killed Keith Moon, then we want some, now!' So we got them and necked them down, washed them down with water. Next thing we know, it was like our noses were on fire and we were all falling about, screaming, 'our noses are on fire, our noses are on fire!' And then everything went blank for 24 hours. When we came to, we wondered what had happened and when we listened back to the recording, we were completely bombed out. We had to re-record everything again as what we had recorded was totally shocking".

I was curious to find out why Mani hadn't surfaced for our interview but was told by Innes that, "He's off scooting". "What?" I replied, having no idea what he meant.

Innes explained that Mani had gone to a local club, which was part of a ritual he undertook wherever he went around the world, he would call up a club and ask if he could come in and scoot with them.

"And what about [lead singer] Bobby Gillespie?" I asked. "Why is he not here?"

"He just can't be fucked" he answered.

After the interview was done, the subject of drugs reared its head again when the tour manager turned to them and said, "drugs are expensive here, $300 for a gram".

Primal Scream originally had a second Melbourne scheduled for later that evening, but the publicist told me that the show was now no longer going ahead. The band made plans to leave Melbourne the next day around lunch time. The publicist later tried desperately, before the band had departed, to get a phone interview organized for me with Mani since he was supposed to be one of the interviewees but no matter how hard he tried, it never came to fruition. She told me that it was the kind crap she had to deal with constantly with a band like Primal Scream.

17 - THE ADVENTURES OF BOOTS ELECTRIC

American combo Eagles Of Death Metal were formed in 1998 by life-long friends vocalist and guitarist Jesse Hughes and drummer Joshua Homme – who is better known as the front man and guitarist with Queens Of The Stone Age and prior to that band, he was guitarist with American stoner rock outfit Kyuss. Both Hughes and Homme have remained constant members of Eagles Of Death Metal, particularly as the primary musicians in the studio, though over the twenty plus years the band has been in existence a number of musicians have passed through its ranks as additional studio musicians and as touring band members. The name does not reflect the style of music the band play which has no relation whatsoever to do with the 'death metal' genre. The music is more akin to a cocktail of swampy blues rock mixed with punky garage topped by sprinklings of glam. The band would later make world headlines when they were caught up in the tragic Bataclan terrorist attack that occurred in Paris in November 2015.

The charismatic Hughes, who goes under several nicknames such as 'The Devil' and 'Boots Electric', has caused quite a stir of controversy with his at times outrageous claims and statements. In March 2007 I met up with Hughes and the rest of the members from the Eagles of Death Metal on their inaugural tour of Australia. The initial connection I made with the band was via a friend at Maton Guitars. On this particular day my friend was heading back from the airport where he had just picked up the band upon their arrival at Tullamarine earlier that morning. While driving back he had put in a call to invite me to join the band while they were in Melbourne for a show. After a brief chat, he handed the phone to both Jesse and the band's touring second guitarist Dave Catching as a way of introducing us. Both greeted me over the phone and told me they were looking forward to catching up with me later in the day.

Just before ending the call, I told them that I had an interview lined up with their support band, Irish retro rockers The Answer who had also arrived in town. So my first stop was The Vibe Hotel in the inner city suburb of Parkville to conduct my interview. The band had recently released a debut album, *Rise*. The traffic in Melbourne was chaotic due to the Grand Prix also being in town. The previous night saw the band play their own show at The Evelyn Hotel, a popular watering hole on Brunswick Street in the artsy environs of inner city Fitzroy which hosted local and international acts seven nights a week.

Once I arrived at The Vibe, I met The Answer's 'driver' in the foyer and we got into some small talk before he escorted me up via the elevator to guitarist Paul Mahon's room. We knocked on and Mahon, who was short in stature, answered the door with just a towel wrapped around him. As he was in the midst of finishing off blow drying his hair, he asked us if we didn't mind waiting for him downstairs as he would join us downstairs shortly after for our.

When he surfaced I found him a truly nice guy and enthusiastic about his band's music. Later, the rest of the band came down to the foyer. Micky Waters (bassist) quickly ventured outside to have a cigarette, while James Heatley (drummer) and Cormac Neeson (lead vocalist) loitered around the foyer. After the interview we spent some time conversing while waiting for the band's tour manager to arrive to take the band to The Palace in St Kilda for their sound check. Originally built in 1972 The Palace would close in a few short months following a fire after which it would sadly be demolished.

I made my way to the venue so I could finally catch up with Eagles of Death Metal. As the band had just come from Japan and would only be in town for the day, they would not have much time to enjoy the locale's delights as they had to catch an early flight the following day for their next show in Brisbane. Once I arrived I waited outside for the band but there was no sighting of Hughes or Catching. Wondering where they were, I asked around before being informed that both were at the doctors, but that they would return soon. Hughes, I was told, had somehow picked up got a viral infection and their tour manager had injured his ankle.

Trying to get inside the venue was a drama in itself. I had trouble getting in due to the fact the venue security and office woman were playing some power games with me. I quickly made a call to my friend who came out and sorted everything out and secured my AAA passes. He then accompanied me to the band's dressing room where I was introduced to the rest of the band. By now Hughes had returned and looked refreshed. His red shoulder length hair was slicked back in a kind of rockabilly style, and his moustache joined freshly grown facial stubble. His sunglasses made him look like the ultimate rock star.

I was introduced to the rest of the touring band; Brian O'Connor (bassist), Catching and Gene Trautmann (drummer). Catching was sitting with a laptop on his knees listening to music on an iPod, while O'Connor eased back into his seat and rolled a joint and began smoking it.

Hughes was busy signing some posters while Trautmann practiced on a small makeshift drum kit. I checked out their rider which consisted of a bottle of Jack Daniels, a bottle of vodka along with a tub of cold beer and a platter of meats, cheeses and various snacks.

The sounds of The Answer sound checking could be through the dressing walls. We all just loitered around the room for a while, conversing before it we went to get some dinner at a nearby street café in St. Kilda's famed Fitzroy Street. Hughes didn't join us until a bit later, as he needed to remain at the venue to do an interview. We were gathered around a large wooden table and took turns looking at the menu and ordering meals and drinks as numerous conversations between us began. Not long after Hughes finally made an appearance and ordered some soup.

Hughes requested I conduct the interview with him there and then, as it provided the perfect opportunity as we all had some time to wait before our meals arrived and were served. I found him a great interviewee; witty, intelligent, friendly, and very accommodating. It was a stark contrast to how the media usually portrayed him. I could best describe Hughes' character and make up as a mishmash of that of a bawdy court jester and charismatic preacher. He's eccentric and in his own words also a 'devout Christian'.

Months earlier the Eagles Of Death Metal had been booted off their opening slot for Guns N' Roses after just one night of a scheduled three week stint when Axl Rose publicly called Hughes' band, "The Pigeons Of Shit Metal". I was curious to find out from Hughes what really went down that night.

"What happened was Guns N' Roses were only into their second song of their set. Now you have to understand that it was a 25,000 seat arena with only 5,000 people there and not one of them was born when *Appetite For Destruction* came out. And they had just got done booing The Suicide Girls, now naked chicks at a rock show getting booed is an absolute fuckin' outrage! Anyway, Axl was into the second song and suddenly he fires the monitor guy and has him kicked out of the building and remember this is his best friend of 25 years! Then he says to the audience, 'what did you think of the "Pigeons of Shit Metal"? You've got to feel sorry for the little fellas, as they're off the tour'. Then [Guns' bassist] Tommy Stinson, in protest at what just happened to us, walked off stage and Axl grabbed his bass and threw it at him. That is the truth, dude. So that is more of a rock 'n' roll outrage. To me, and I'm not going to lie to you man, having one of my idols insult me and make fun of me from the same stage that I accepted and shared with them, is a very hurtful thing. It's also a classless, mean thing that is beneath someone who should be of that stature. But I learned a lesson, which is that people can all make the wrong choices and ruin themselves. Axl is like the white Michael Jackson of rock 'n' roll, who is singing music in the best paid karaoke band ever. Guns N' Roses really became Velvet Revolver that's where the rock 'n' roll went, man".

After the incident Hughes said Rose's management called his manager to apologize and offered the band back their remaining dates opening for Guns N' Roses but Hughes stood firm and declined saying, "He [Rose] can go fuck himself".

Pretty soon everyone around the table was joining in with the conversation and some women joined the band at the table who seemed to have got to know them already. At one point a handful of fans strolled past, and stopped upon recognizing Hughes and asked if they could take some photos with him and sign some stuff for them to which Hughes obliged.

After our meal we made our way back to the venue. As it was a cool evening in Melbourne it made for an enjoyable stroll. Again Hughes was approached by many fans along the way as they were heading to the show, and all asked for photos with him. Hughes loved the attention, so always obliged. He made mentioned to us that as he was walking out of the venue earlier, he made sure to mingle with each and every fan that had lined up to enter the venue.

As show time drew nearer, everyone started getting changed into their stage outfits. Hughes tried on a gold cape, which made him look like a super hero from a comic book. The sweet smell of weed permeated the air. It was a relaxed atmosphere, and a couple of female friends of the band came in and chatted before heading back out.

While the band prepared for the show, I made my way out to the side of the stage to check out The Answer who were now rocking the crowd. The band sounded tight and powerful and the songs were going down well with the audience. After a while I returned to the dressing room, where Hughes showed us a cool watch given to him by a French company for some advertising he had done for them. He told us that they gave him a stack to keep. He pulled out a small bottle of eye drops which he said he received from a doctor in Japan. He explained that when he dropped them in his eyes, they would sting like hell but once the sting subsided his eyes felt refreshed.

Hughes looked over the set list and explained to one of the crew about watching his cue for when he puts on the cape for the segment in the show. O'Connor, who wore a bowler hat, shared the story of how a similar hat he had got stolen recently. He told me he had bought it in London on a recent visit but somehow a fan ended up stealing it from him. The particular fan then went onto My Space and told him that she had the hat and that if O'Connor wanted it back he had to give her two tickets to a show! O'Connor refused to give in to her demands, and just told her to get lost and went out and bought another hat.

Six months later Hughes made a return visit to Melbourne, though this time he was travelling solo courtesy of Maton Guitars who had brought him out in order to engage him in some promotional activities. Over the course of a few days whilst he'd been in Melbourne, it had seen him judge a competition where he'd given away a Maton guitar as part of a prize and undertaken numerous press appearances. I was again invited to meet up with him on one of the days, where I was instructed to meet Hughes in the early afternoon at Sing Sing recording studios in the inner Melbourne suburb of Richmond.

As I walked toward the studio, a car with Hughes in the passenger seat pulled up at a parking bay near the entrance. Hughes got out and noticing me came over and gave me a friendly hug and just like the last time he was fully "on" and obviously slightly loaded as he was smoking a joint, the vapours permeating the air from his car. As he took one last drag we entered the studio together. Hughes quickly told me how Eagles Of Death Metal were public enemy number one on a Christian website that had recently decried the band as endorsers of gay lifestyles. Hughes told me his mother did a lot of online stuff and had told her son about the site. I asked him how he felt about it. "If you take too much notice of what's written about you, it'll do your head in," he replied.

Once inside Hughes asked the studio manager if he

could take a look around as he was interested in recording an album there. In one of the recording rooms a band was tracking some material. It transpired that Hughes had been out on the town the previous night and met members of local electro-rock outfit Dukes Of Windsor, who had invited him to come into the studio and lay down some backing vocals for a track the band were working on. The Dukes of Windsor were at Sing Sing Studios recording a new single which they hoped to put out to radio in the coming few weeks and in stores soon after. We were escorted to the control room where the band were listening to a playback. Greetings were exchanged and before Hughes went into the vocal booth, he began looking around the studio with some of the band joining him on a studio tour. Hughes was impressed and fell in love with the studio, especially the ambience of the rooms and the recording consoles. An old Farfisa organ sat in one corner of one of the studio while a piano sat in another.

While Hughes looked I walked outside. Wearing an old pair of track suit pants and looking a little worse for wear, Shane Howard – singer-songwriter from Australian 1980s band Goanna - was standing outside nearby and I introduced myself. He told me he was taking a smoke break from producing the new album by Archie Roach - one of Australia's most respected Indigenous musicians - at the studio. Roach was sitting outside in the glorious spring sunshine on the courtyard taking a break as well. The album *Journey* was released in October that year.

We discussed Goanna's *Spirit of Place* album, which Howard informed me would be celebrating 25 years old later that year (November) and that he now lived about four and half hours away near the coastal town of Apollo Bay in Victoria so travelled the long distance to Melbourne for his work. Soon it was time to return back inside, he to his recording and I to Hughes' session.

As I re-entered the room, Dukes Of Windsor's lead vocalist Jack Weaving was busy instructing Hughes what he would like him to do on the song while the recording engineer prepared to press record. Weaving and Hughes both headed into the vocal booth and laid down the vocals parts. They ran through the song a few times and did a few takes.

Weaving then asked Hughes if he could do another vocal part. Inspired, Hughes grabbed a pen and wrote some lyrics down and both he and Weaving went into the vocal booth again and did some further backing vocals. Hughes seemed to be having so much fun. He lit up the room with his infectious humour. Still wearing his trademark 'rock star' shades, he quickly switched them for a pair of Buddy Holly spectacles.

He recalled a time when a certain flirtation with a blonde didn't go to plan. "We were playing a ladies only show in Soho and before the gig I was walking up and down the hallway while we were setting our stuff up and one of the hottest blonde girls I've ever seen in my life was standing in the door way. She was just standing there talking to her boy. So I start making eyes at her and I get a look back. Then I get the balls to talk to her and I go up and I am flirting with her but she's not saying a word to me. So I go, 'hey what's up, are you staying to see the show tonight?' And still no word. Then I go 'so what's your name?' and she finally goes 'my name's Lloyd'. Lloyd was a fuckin' dude!"

He also put on a pair of black gloves, he told all of us they were authentic police gloves that were specially made for searches and could prevent syringe punches and knives

Enjoying dinner together with EODM's Jesse Hughes at The Jam Factory, South Yarra, 2007.

from penetrating. Then he began to tell dirty jokes, which caused further laughter to spread all around the room. He then revealed the true nature of the gloves by sharing even more raunchy stories.

After the hysterics he and I headed outside to search for something to eat. I asked him about his friendship with Josh Homme and his own documented sex escapades. All the while, he continued smoking a joint and getting high. We then decided it would be easier to head to Chapel Street, to a nearby food and entertainment precinct in South Yarra. We jumped into our cars and set off. We met up again in the car park of The Jam Factory, and walked down Chapel Street, all the while, he was still puffing away on the remaining fragments of his joint. I asked him about how heavy he got with drugs, "I like doing speed" he revealed, "I'm always on so speed helps to chill me out".

I asked him about Lemmy from Motorhead. "He's a nice guy and we share the same dealer who sells us speed. They don't call Lemmy the mayor of Hollywood for nothing!" I asked him about his lady friends and whether he had them falling in love? "I keep them very close. We all like to love and I like romance so I take them out to dinner but once in the bedroom, I like to....". He also admitted that the previous night he had enjoyed a ménage à trois!

As we walked along the street he spotted a Lee jeans store and asked that we go inside. I followed him in and he looked around and tried on some tight fitting jeans. "I'm a size 29 waist" he said. A young female shop assistant served him as he tried the pair of jeans on. She asked him who he was. "I am Jesse from Eagles Of Death Metal" he replied.

"Oh my God, my boyfriend is going to be wrapped".

After Hughes came out from the change room, he began charming a small group of women who had entered the store. As he went to finalize his purchase, it dawned on him that he had left his credit card back at his hotel. He asked the shop assistant if she could hold the jeans for him along with a pink shirt he had picked out, and told her he would return for them the next day. She obliged and as a thank you, Hughes signed an autograph for her, and then offered up an invite for her and a friend to come to a party in his hotel room later that night. He also gave her his room number and phone number!

Leaving the store we walked to a food court nearby for some Singapore noodles where he shared further war stories. After dinner Hughes was eager for me to listen to three demo tracks of a new Eagles Of Death Metal album that was in the process of being recorded. So pulled his iPod out and a set of headphones, and I gave the tracks a listen. They sounded great to my ears: one had a T-Rex groove, while another was very dance-y while the other was your typical Eagles Of Death Metal rock tune. I liked what I heard. The album *Heart On* would eventually be released in 2008.

18 - ALL THAT GLITTERS

Glam rock's early purveyors such as Marc Bolan and T-Rex, Slade, Gary Glitter and The Sweet, set the scene for the genre's popularity over the early years of the 1970s. Glam Rock, also known as Glitter Rock, had a formula that was simple, flamboyant, loud and relied heavily on stomping beats and huge guitar riffs. The genre struck a chord with every teenage girl and boy and dominated the music scene before it came to an end around the middle of the decade as the early strains of punk became more and more popular and fashionable.

1977 saw a changing of the guard, and with punk firmly gripping the scene Glam was done. Marc Bolan's tragic demise in a car accident in September of that year was the final nail in the coffin. Bolan's legacy would live beyond his death and many bands over the years would go on and name check him as an influence. Today, at the crash site of his death a memorial stands. Located on Queen's Ride near Gipsy Lane in Barnes in South West London, it's a five minute walk from nearby Barnes railway station. Fans from all over the world regularly make a pilgrimage to the site. During one of my European tours, I too visited Bolan's memorial. On the day I visited I was the sole visitor, so in peace, I was able to pay my respects alone. A notice board erected at the site nearby was covered in pictures, drawings, cards and personal messages, with some having faded due to the passage of time.

Over the years I managed to interview and meet several of Glam Rock's favourite sons and daughters such as Suzi

Quatro, Roxy Music and The Sweet. My first interview with a Glam rock great was on a warm Tuesday evening in January 2006 when I put in a call to the queen of the genre herself, Suzi Quatro, who was doing pre-release interviews for her new studio album *Back To The Drive* which was scheduled for release in March of that year. The new album saw a return to form for Quatro revisiting her spirited 70's heyday and creative peak. With production work by her and The Sweet's Andy Scott and Steve Grant it garnered a favourable reception from fans and critics.

Quatro has been a frequent visitor to Australian shores over the years where the leather-clad, bass-wielding rocker has been able to sustain a solid following and remain hugely popular. Since her first visit down under in May 1974, she's undertaken over 30 tours. On this occasion, she was only doing phone interviews as she wasn't touring Australia that year, though would be the following year in support of the new album.

At the time Quatro was fifty-five years old, and was still as driven and enthused about her music as ever. As was the case with all my interview preparations, I would spend days researching and many hours listening to her new album so that I totally understood the artist and the music. This rigorous approach has always stood me in good stead. Quatro was really impressed that I knew so much about the album and had listened to it. In fact she told me, "Thank God, a journalist with a brain!" after I told her that 'Duality', one of the songs on the album, summed up the entire album, an album that revealed her two sides that represent the twin aspects of her astrological birth star sign Gemini; the soft rock and hard rock sides to her musical personality. I won her over from that moment on.

Credited as being the first major female rock star,

Detroit-born Quatro started her career in an all-female rock band called The Pleasure Seekers that also included two of Quatro's sisters in the line-up. She eventually moved to England to pursue a solo career in 1971 and released her self-titled debut album, though in Australia it was renamed and issued as *Can The Can*, in 1973 which set Quatro onto the road to international success and popularity. During the interview we discussed the new album but she was happy to look back over her career.

I asked her whether there was any truth to the rumour that she couldn't wear any panties and bras underneath any of the leather cat suits she wore during the 1970s.

"You actually couldn't" she replied. "Because the line of the jumpsuit was so skin tight, you didn't want any lines showing. Anyway, I'm a small busted girl so a bra didn't really look right on me anyway."

Did she ever indulge in the excesses of rock 'n' roll like drugs I asked?

"I got to say, I always found drugs boring. Of course I tried them but only very early on, but I didn't like it and I just did not like getting high".

What about groupies?

"I was with Len Tuckey then – her guitarist and later husband – but I always had groupies of both sexes and still do. In fact one particular guy was the reason I wrote 'Glycerine Queen'."

As the interview neared its end, I told her that I was doing the phone interview from inside my studio and had one of my guitars next me, and asked if she wouldn't mind if she sang me a few lines from one of my favourite Quatro songs, 'Michael' while I strummed away on the guitar? She kindly obliged and went ahead and sung a few lines while I accompanied her on my guitar over the phone. To my ears it sounded fantastic. It made my evening. I've always thought that 'Michael' was a highly under-rated and over looked ballad which appeared on her third studio album, *Your Mamma Won't Like Me* in 1975, and was released as a single in Australia. I thanked her for her time and the little sing-a-long and hoped to catch her show when she toured Australia the next time.

Though Roxy Music started out as Glam rockers, they quickly morphed into something more sophisticated, in turn inspiring an art-rock movement all of their own, one which was a major influence on the New Wave and New Romantic genres that emerged from the late 1970s to early 1980s.

I've always been a fan of Roxy. I first got into their music when I was in my last year of primary school in 1976 when their song, 'Love Is The Drug' became a big hit in Australia. I then followed their career until their eventual split in 1983 after they had released their last studio album, *Avalon,* a year earlier. In 2001 the group reunited until their demise once again after their 2011 Australian tour. In fact, the seven shows the band performed in Australia in February and March 2011 were the final Roxy Music performances to date. Prior to the that tour the band had last been in Australia back in August 2001 as part of the original reunion tour.

I was looking forward to their 2011 visit to Australia. I had interviewed Roxy Music guitarist Phil Manzanera over the phone the previous year as part of a feature I wrote on him for an English guitar magazine, and after our interview he kindly invited me to Roxy Music's Melbourne show when they were in town the following year to finally meet him backstage after the show.

Roxy Music arrived in Melbourne as part of their *For Your Pleasure* world tour on Thursday March 3 2011. Upon arriving at Rod Laver Arena I was informed by one of the promotions company people that there were sadly only around 4,500 people in attendance, so the arena looked a little more empty than usual. With my tickets affording me the best view of the show, and as the stage lights dimmed and the audience's cheers increased in volume, the band walked out onstage at 8:30pm to the sounds of the instrumental 'India' piping through the PA system. Present were original members; Phil Manzanera (guitar), Bryan Ferry (vocals), Andy McKay (saxophone) and Paul Thompson (drums). The band was rounded out by a few extra touring members that included 22 year-old guitar wiz kid Oliver Thompson on guitar and Bryan Ferry's son Tara Ferry on percussion.

As they positioned themselves with their respective instruments, they kicked off the night's show with 'The Main Thing'. While Phil started the set with his signature Gibson Firebird, in between songs he switched from Dave Gilmour's Black Fender Strat to a three-pick-up Gibson Les Paul before returning to his Firebird again to end the night's set. Though for Oliver Thompson, he mainly played a Black Les Paul throughout the show.

Bryan Ferry didn't say much during the whole set and during the first few numbers it seemed like he was struggling, as if he wanted to get through the songs as quickly as possible. Midway things did pick up and once the 'Same Old Scene' kicked off, the crowd were on their feet dancing. 'Let's Stick Together' really pumped the crowd to a new height. Oliver did a number of cool guitar solos and Phil undertook some cool ones himself. The group performed against a backdrop of an ever-changing set of visuals with the players themselves blending into the visuals at various points throughout the set.

During the last refrain of the final song, 'For Your Pleasure', one by one, each of the band's members left the stage and waved goodbye to the audience as they each walked off stage, starting with Bryan Ferry first until pianist Colin Good was the last to walk off to the echoing last strains of sounds emanating from his piano. No encore was played. It had just gone 10.20pm.

Setlist for the night was: India (tape, for walk on) - The Main Thing - Street Life - Pyjamarama - Prairie Rose - If There Is Something - More Than This - Jealous Guy - Like A Hurricane - 2HB - In Every Dream Home A Heartache - Tara - Bitter Sweet - To Turn You On - Same Old Scene - My Only Love - Virginia Plain - Love Is The Drug - Editions Of You - Do The Strand - Avalon - Let's Stick Together- For Your Pleasure.

Once the show was over I made my way backstage. Claire Singers (Phil's lovely wife who also doubled as his PR agent) had earlier issued me with a couple of backstage passes so I had brought a friend along with me for the evening. While waiting around to be escorted backstage, a couple of women strolled past, took one look at my passes and told the security who was manning the backstage entrance, "We are with this guy!" and in jest grabbed my arm as though they were coming with me backstage. Soon after a familiar face came into view, Janick Gers, the guitarist from heavy metal band Iron Maiden who was casually walking around the perimeter of the arena. Coincidentally, Iron Maiden were in town for the Soundwave festival.

Finally, the moment had arrived, and we were ushered into the backstage area along with about 20 other invited guests. While we waited for the band to appear in one of the spacious rooms set aside for the band and guests, everyone was treated to free beers. A few moments later a couple of the band members walked in followed by Phil and Claire. As soon as I spotted Phil I greeted him with, "Hey Phil, I'm Joe". I tried to shake his hand but he had a wine bottle and a couple glasses in his hands. He put them down and shook my hand in return. Phil then introduced me to Claire as well.

First thing Phil said to me was, "Joe! How are you? I love your instrumental track 'Travellin' West'. Very cool, it's something I would do". That made my night! I had the previous year officially released my debut instrumental 'Travellin' West' a multi-layered acoustic outing and sent Phil a copy. Hearing such a compliment coming from a guitarist and artist of his calibre meant the world to me. I thanked him for the compliment and added, "I'll send you some more then".

"Now, don't get too carried away" he replied jokingly, and we both burst out laughing.

Phil and I chatted for a while, talking shop and about the evening's performance. I brought up the subject of the Dave Gilmour Strat, as well as Oliver's playing. Phil told me Oliver was a friend of Bryan's son Tara and that he had also played on Bryan's album. Then I asked him how he was enjoying being in Australia. He said that both he and Claire and were enjoying it immensely. "Today we went to Lorne, and it was great" he said. I mentioned how much I loved his *Diamond Head* album from 1975 and he told me how the reissue that had recently come out was garnering some great reviews in the UK press. We talked a bit more, before he had to move onto to catching up with some other people in the room who were waiting for him. I asked him for a guitar pick to add to my collection and he pulled one from his pocket. I thanked him for the passes and opportunity to meet him and hung around for a little while longer enjoying the moment and hospitality. The memory of that evening remains.

The Sweet enjoyed several years of popularity during the 1970s both during Glam Rock's reign and a few years after when they became unlikely heroes of the nascent punk scene. However ever since the hits dried up the band maintained a hectic touring schedule keeping their legacy and the music alive.

I met the band for the first time in 2004 when the band toured Australia when I interviewed The Sweet's mainstay guitarist Andy Scott in a suburban pub on the afternoon of their show. Casually dressed, and enjoying one of the local brews, Scott and I chatted for about half an hour which covered varied topics from the band's past to the present day. The show later that evening was standing room only and the band had clearly lost none of their appeal to hardcore fans.

The next time I caught up with them was during my *Slave To The Fingers* European Tour in 2012. I had finished the last leg of my tour in London and had a few days free before my return to Australia. I flew over to Hamburg, to peruse the sights and sounds of the city and catch up with both The Sweet and another fellow 1970s English act Smokie on the last day of my stay.

Though Smokie were never what you could term Glam, their early hits including their 1976 signature hit 'Living Next Door To Alice' written by Glam hit songwriting duo Nicky Chinn and Mike Chapman. The pair also wrote hits for Suzi Quatro, The Sweet and others. Around late afternoon I caught up with them at the Radisson Hotel, a short distance from Hamburg Airport, where the band was holed up. I spent the next four hours sat at the hotel's restaurant bar with Terry Uttley, long-time bass player with Smokie, who shared war stories with us and showed us family and holiday photos on his phone.

Smokie were headlining an arena show under the title of *Oldie* put on by the German public radio broadcasting station NDR 90.3 at the 'Alsterdorfer Sporthalle' in the northern part of Hamburg. Along with Smokie, the other performers appearing on the same bill for the evening's show included The Sweet, The Rubettes featuring Alan Williams, Boney M, Pussycat and several other legendary recording hit makers from the 1970s. With a AAA pass both myself and Alex Wieser from Austria-based record label W.A.R Productions, to whom I was signed at the time, spent considerable time backstage and in the bands' dressing rooms meeting the acts. When we arrived around 9pm the final strains of 'Sugar Baby Love' performed by The Rubettes' Alan Williams could be heard and the deafening sounds of applause echoed across the enormous sports hall.

Later, having enjoyed a smorgasbord dinner in the backstage canteen, we made our way to The Sweet's dressing room and passed Liz Mitchell from Boney M, who had already performed their set, standing in the hallway chatting away to one of the promoter's personnel. The Sweet at that time had the line-up of guitarist Andy Scott with Pete Lincoln on lead vocals and bass, Bruce Bisland on drums and Tony O'Hora on triple duties as second guitarist, keyboards and backing vocals.

While each band had their very own dressing room,

with Smokie's being the largest of the lot, The Sweet's was tiny in comparison. With Scott nowhere to be found the remaining members; Bisland, O'Hora and Lincoln were making the best out of a very small space and we chatted away until we moved onto Smokie's dressing room where Uttley was being interviewed by one of the NDR people, while Smokie guitarist Mick McConnell – who had also played guest guitar solos on two of my early instrumental outings - had changed into his stage clothes and sat with his guitar doing some pre-show finger exercises. The rest of the band were also changing into their stage garb.

As The Sweet prepared to hit the stage we made our way out and took our seat in one of the VIP areas at the side of the stage. Each band played a great set, but the sound wasn't the best. The 7,000 seat arena was sold-out but after The Sweet had completed their set people began leaving, as the audience was largely comprised of a demographic old enough to remember the original bands in the 1970s, while the rest waited patiently for Smokie to take to the stage for the final performance of the night. The band eventually hit the stage rather late, but by this time the remaining audience had dwindled by about half.

The third time I caught The Sweet was on their 2014 Australian tour. By this time Lincoln had also guested on my track 'Shining Star' playing bass. Sadly Tony's wife was battling breast cancer and just days before the band was due to fly out of the UK, Tony announced that he would not be joining Sweet on the Australian leg of this tour. Tony was replaced by Paul Manzi. I caught the band's show in Shepparton, a regional rural city about a 30 minute drive form my hometown of Kyabram. After the show I met up with Lincoln and due to Tony's situation it was a sombre affair. In February 2017 Scott returned to Australia as part of supergroup QSP which comprised three of Glam's greats: Scott on guitar and vocals, Quatro on vocals and bass and Slade drummer Don Powell. Their show at Hamer Hall showcased the band's debut album as support act for Quatro's own show as headliner as part of her *Australian Leather Forever – Encore* Tour.

19 - HOLD ON, HOLD OUT

The first time I met American singer/songwriter and guitar wielding popster-cum-bluesman John Mayer was in June 2002 in Melbourne. He was only 24 at the time and was on his very first ever promo visit of Australia. Previously he'd released his major label debut *Room For Squares* in 2001 but it was a slow burner, especially in Australia but then it got a major push from his label Sony Music in 2002 and from then on, as they say, the rest is history. On that first night in Melbourne we had been invited to an intimate showcase he was performing, organized by his record label with the sole purpose of introducing him to the Australian media showcasing material from his debut album. There weren't many of us in the small bar in the centre of Melbourne that night which might have been because it was a Sunday night or more likely because at that point no one had heard of John Mayer.

As Mayer played his tunes the vibe in the room was less than warm, as most seemed totally neutral to it all. When John got to the end of his set he sensed that he had failed to garner the attention of those in attendance and changed tack by playing a cover of American blues guitar legend Stevie Ray Vaughan's instrumental 'Lenny'. As soon as he started playing it the mood in the room changed. Suddenly everyone sat up and took notice. In one fell swoop he had won everyone over. His mastery of the guitar, particularly of the blues genre, was very much evident. I and everyone else in that room knew in that moment that everything would change for him... and it did. Within months his album became a hit and was all over radio and on the charts. He would return for his first proper Australian tour later that year where he played to sold-out shows.

The first time I interviewed John was the next day after that initial debut performance at the Como Hotel in upmarket South Yarra. Walking into the Como that day the first thing I encountered was Mayer sat at the piano tickling the ivories, improvising and singing:

"I don't mind the comparisons/ to Dave Matthews, it's just fine/ I know the life I've got in my hands/ Room For Squares is a record that's coming out/ it's already come out in Australia/... yeah, yeah, oh, oh...I'm going to play piano!"

I applauded his impromptu performance, it was certainly a great way to break the ice! Moving off the piano chair I noticed he was tall, well over six feet. The comparisons he mentioned were in relation to reviews that likened him to acoustic rocker Dave Matthews. We took a seat and the first thing I asked him was about his previous night's showcase and how the mood in the room completely changed with that final song. He told me that he hated getting off stage and feeling he hadn't hit it, so on the spur-of-the-moment he decided to add that song which turned things around. So having taken that one last shot, it proved to be a winner for him.

He had a friendly and open disposition and we both enjoyed the interview. We chatted about all things guitars and his debut record. He really loved talking about blues players such as Stevie Ray Vaughan, who was his idol. He said he had come across him after he had been learning to play guitar for about a year. It inspired him to study the blues as prior to that he was playing a lot of metal stuff. At the time of our interview he was planning his next record and desperately wanted to prove himself and be taken seriously as a musician. "I want to establish the trust, consistency and longevity of putting out a lot of records that maintain the same level of quality" he stated at the time, "and to be an exciting live performer". In later years this statement would become somewhat void when Mayer's predilection for celebrity girlfriends and at times, controversial comments, would overshadow his music and guitar prowess.

That interview ended up being published in *Total Guitar* magazine, December 2002 issue in the UK. It was the very first guitar interview ever published of John Mayer anywhere in the UK, a fact confirmed later. When Mayer returned for his first Australian tour in October 2002 on the back of the success of his debut album, I interviewed him again.

We met at the Radisson opposite the historic Flagstaff Gardens, the oldest park in Melbourne having first been established in 1862. As I waited for John and the Sony rep to arrive I started chatting to one of the road crew who told me he was Mayer's drum tech. I asked how things were going and he told me that after they leave Melbourne they would be returning to the US (they had just come from a UK tour) where they would spend a few days rehearsing before heading out on a US tour later that month.

The Sony rep finally arrived with Mayer who quickly remembered our previous interview describing in exact detail our first meeting saying that he had also read it. He even recalled where our first interview took place; at one of the top floors of the Como Hotel and that it was also for a guitar magazine. I was impressed he actually remembered.

As we took our seats in a quiet area of the hotel, I handed him a copy of *Australian Musician* magazine which had quotes taken from that earlier interview and he began to read it. After a minute or two, he looked at me and commented that it was the first time he had seen the name of Stevie Ray Vaughan written correctly in print! As he relaxed he opened up and shared many great stories with a couple verging on the personal. At one point he rolled up his shirt sleeve and showed me some new tattoos he had gotten since our last meeting and his plans to get more.

After the interview he told his Australian record label how much he enjoyed talking guitars with me, this would hold me in good stead for any future interviews as it ensured I'd be granted an interview on his next tour. I found Mayer very passionate about guitar playing in general, and he had a strong desire to keep evolving as a musician and our conversations were always punctuated by his wit and humour. Later that evening I went to his sold-out show at the Hi Fi Bar. We were given the best view in the upstairs area. He came on with a full band in tow around 9:30pm and played a brilliant two-hour set.

About a year later, in September 2003, I got to interview him for a third time. He was again in town touring, this time behind his second album *Heavier Things* which had come out several weeks prior. This time the interview was conducted at the stylish Quay West Hotel in Melbourne's Southbank, the improving quality of the hotels he was staying on each visit corresponded with his upward career trajectory. Having arrived in early afternoon I eventually waited for about an hour as all of his interviews were running behind schedule. Eventually he surfaced after just having finished an interview with Molly Meldrum of *Countdown* fame, for his 'Drum TV' music segment. Meldrum walked out at the same time with Mayer, and I was introduced to him. As soon as Mayer laid eyes on me he told me yet again he remembered our previous interviews and again mentioned the locations of both. I was stoked because out of all the people he had met and spoken to since that first initial interview 18 months earlier he still remembered our conversations.

Before we went to do our interview, he was informed by his publicist that he had one more to do before mine and directed him into another room but as he did so he turned to his label rep and stated excitedly, "I love talking guitars with Joe!" After that interview was done it was my turn – I told him that I was only granted one ticket to his sold-out show later that evening and asked him if it would be possible to get another ticket so that I could bring my then girlfriend, now wife, Liz along to the show? "Leave it with me, we'll arrange it" he said and I ended up with two extra tickets! It seemed success hadn't changed him at that point.

Later that evening Australian pop-rockers Lo-Tel were played a great opening set in support with songs from their newly released album, *The Lost Thing*. Mayer hit the stage at 9pm to hysterical screams from an audience largely comprised of women reminiscent of the kind of hysteria wrought by The Beatles decades earlier. During the set he played an extended solo during *Come Back To Bed* which conjured up the spirit of his guitar hero Stevie Ray Vaughan. The show proved a smashing success, and he came out for an encore, finally wrapping up the show around 10:30pm. Most of his Australian shows had been sold out for weeks in advance, it was a great way to end the evening's entertainment. A few weeks later his Australian record label Sony Music presented me with a special large block mount of the album cover of *Heavier Things* that was personally signed by John as a thank you for my passionate support of him over the past couple of years. This would be the last time I interviewed Mayer, as by the time his next album *Continuum,* in 2006, he was slowly falling into all the trappings fame and fortune had began to bestow him. Toxic behaviour coupled with celebrity girlfriends that ran the gamut from Jennifer Aniston to Jennifer Love Hewitt to Taylor Swift along with his habitual smart-mouthing continually landed him in hot water with both media and public alike over the next few years. The once shy and avowed teetotaller with an anti-drug stance, was lost in a sea of wine, women and song.

An eventual backlash led Mayer to relocate to the American countryside and into self-imposed exile for a number of years, forcing him to self-reflect and slow down away from the glare of the public eye. When he resurfaced, he appeared a changed man, one who had seemingly matured and had learned grace and humility. He even admitted in several interviews later how his thirst in the early years for fame and all the opportunities success afforded him had turned him into a hedonistic behemoth. As he approaches middle age, hopefully this change in Mayer is a return to the guy I knew all those years ago.

Jackson Browne is a quintessential singer-songwriter who, during the course of his career, personified the American West Coast sound and mind set. Though 1972's 'Doctor My Eyes' gave him his first hit song, it was The Eagles' classic 'Take It Easy' (1972) that he co-wrote with Glenn Frey that not only launched The Eagles, but also provided Browne with a massive boost in attention and popularity. His fifth album, 1977's *Running On Empty,* which gave a vivid snapshot of life on the road, brought Browne much acclaim and commercial success. As a writer of deeply introspective songs down the intervening decades, his song writing tended towards a socio-political bent.

Browne has visited Australia quite regularly over the course of his fifty-year career. I first interviewed him when he was on his fifth tour of Australia in 2003. He had recently released his most recent studio album – his twelfth to date – *The Naked Ride Home* at the tail end of 2002. He was staying at the upmarket Como Hotel in South Yarra, which was where my scheduled interview with him took place in early February 2003. An early riser, he had a heavily booked day and as is usually the case they were running a little behind schedule by the time I arrived for my 10:30am appointment and it was another hour before I finally got to interview him. His publicist was busily handling the press schedule on the day, so while I was biding my time, I was introduced to Browne's manager, Donald "Buddha" Miller who told me that Browne was on his second day of interviews and hadn't finished yesterdays until 6:30pm! He also shared stories about Browne's recent shows that had him supporting Tom Petty, which was rare as Browne rarely opened for anybody. It was quite a revealing conversation. He told me that since my interview with Browne would focus more on the technical aspects of music such as guitars and songwriting, he was looking forward to it.

Browne was on a tight schedule as he had to fly out of Melbourne later that same day at 5pm to go to New Zealand as he had some shows to do there first before returning to Australia in a few weeks' time. We were lost in conversation when finally the moment came, and I got my first glimpse of Browne as he entered the hotel lobby.

Then aged 54, he looked younger than that and

during the interview he just talked and talked and talked. Whenever he spoke he always looked me straight in the eye, and sipped on water during our entire chat. He seemed very relaxed and was a great interviewee. I had prepared a lot of questions but cut out many of them, as I wanted to allow the interview to move forward at its own pace.

I was curious about how he felt being credited with spearheading the whole 1970s West Coast singer-songwriter scene. "I'm a product of the values of that time so I don't think of myself as starting anything" he told me before pausing to gather his thoughts and then added, "I'm really just the continuation of certain values that are very much alive today in other great singer-songwriters. I basically grew up listening to Bob Dylan, The Beatles, The Rolling Stones and a lot of folk music. At the same time I was listening to The Beatles, I was listening to Tom Paxton, Howlin' Wolf, Mississippi John Hurt, Pete Seeger and Judy Collins. In the same moment in time that I was listening to 'Strawberry Fields Forever', I was also listening to Leonard Cohen, you know, so that's the product I came out of. They were the people that came right before me and I think they're the greatest songwriters of our time and particularly Mississippi John Hurt the Delta blues man who was an amazing, original stylist". After just half an hour our time was up and it was time for Browne to move onto his next scheduled interview.

A few weeks later, I attended his Melbourne show where I ran into the Warner Music publicist again and we chatted briefly, he told me Browne's show that evening would feature songs spanning his entire career over a two hour set. He mentioned having witnessed the sound check earlier which went for about an hour and shared the fact that the following day's show at Rochford Wines as part of *A Day On The Green*, had already amassed 5,000 ticket sales. Browne hit the stage to a full house at 9pm as loud applause echoed across the theatre and with his six-piece band in tow: two guitarists, a drummer, a keyboardist, bassist and percussionist and kicked off with 'Somebody's Baby'. The next two hours were like a trip down memory lane, with Jackson in fine form and his voice as strong as ever. He gave good banter in between songs and talked about the situation with the Iraq War and how he believed the public were not to believe what the media were telling us in Australia that all Americans were in favour of it. He also shared the story of how he marched in a peace rally alongside his son in Sydney the week prior as his son lived there.

Later he was joined on stage by Australia's soul queen Renee Geyer for one song – she was the support act for the evening. Jackson mainly played rhythm guitar and piano during the set. The show saw him do three encores that included 'Load Out/Stay' which incorporated the audience clapping and singing along. The finale was a guitar duelling extravaganza, where his guitarists did an extended jam, trading solos. The sound and light show was fantastic and when he finally left the stage, he left the crowd hungry for more.

In April 2004 Jackson returned for another Australian tour, this time an acoustic solo tour. It was a good crowd for the performance held in the plush seated Regent Theatre. This particular show was actually the second that was added after the first one (which was the following evening's show) sold out. This time Browne came on just after 8pm and played for over an hour and a half. The setting was fairly sparse, just 14 acoustic guitars and an electric piano the only instruments forming the stage's setting. With no pre-arranged set list Browne took the spontaneous route, allowing the audience to request the tunes instead, which he then proceeded to play. Casually attired, it fitted perfectly within the intimate and spontaneous spirit of the show. There was a brief intermission half way through. He was later joined onstage again by Renee Geyer for a song. Browne explained how he first heard of Geyer through his good friend Bonnie Raitt. The stories he shared in between songs were fascinating and entertaining. One anecdote was about the many different cover versions of 'Take It Easy' that had been recorded over the years and in different languages. In particularly he singled out one version that was recorded in Chinese which he admitted he had yet to hear, and was very curious to hear what it actually sounded like. His guitar playing on the night was good, and he accompanied himself very well and played some great guitar licks in certain songs.

Browne told another story about touring Australia at the same time as Bob Dylan for the Melbourne Blues Festival the year before. Browne had gone to Dylan's show and watched him from the side of the stage. Browne was astounded how Dylan didn't say a word to the fans during the whole show. He contrasted this story, recalling a time in Florida in the 1960s when he made the error of being vocal about the local police force which resulted in him being escorted from the venue. Browne's manager at the time later told him to "never interact with the audience". Thankfully he never adhered to that rule over the course of his career and as if to highlight this when one member of the audience persistently kept calling out for 'For A Dancer' Browne gave in to the fan's request and closed his performance with it.

Two years later, in April 2006, he returned to Australia

repeating the previous acoustic show format but this time Browne had mainstay guitarist David Lindley by his side. Hamer Hall provided the perfect setting with its fine modern decor and artsy stylistics. This tour would culminate in Browne's performance at the East Coast International Blues and Roots Festival in Byron Bay over Easter weekend.

For the opener, 'For Everyman', Browne was seated with acoustic guitar in his hand and flanked on his left by David Lindley on guitar (Lindley also alternated between lap steel, bouzouki, fiddle and Oud on selected songs) and percussionist Luis Conte on his right. The resonating of the acoustics and soothing percussion created the perfect ambience which permeated to the depths of your inner being. It brought a power and depth to Browne's songs, exposing them in their most intimate form. The trio were back dropped by a long line of acoustic guitars. During the performance Browne kept up a playful chatter with both Conte and Lindley which occasionally spilled out into the audience as well.

The heavily thick set and side-burned Lindley was dressed in a multi coloured polyester shirt at which Browne remarked "David is the king of polyester!" he also added that he often tried to match Lindley's wardrobe and in fact, for the current tour, had bought some shirts to wear on stage but just couldn't bring himself to wear them. During the set Browne performed a good selection of material spanning his entire career such as 'These Days' - introduced by Browne as "the first song David and I played together" – 'Carmelita', which he prefaced as saying was written by Warren Zevon, the long standing classic 'Take It Easy', 'The Barricades of Heaven', 'Running On Empty' and a couple of tracks off Lindley's solo album *El Rayo X*;

the track 'Mercury Blues' - introduced by Browne as "a song about a car" and the title track 'El Rayo-X'.

Similar to his last acoustic show, he interspersed his onstage banter with the occasional anecdote, my favourite of which revolved around the time Browne was making a record with his band and on one particular recording he had to call Luis back in to the studio because one of his 'beats' was out of time. Conte wouldn't believe it. Conte came into the studio's control room so he could be shown exactly where the 'beats' were supposedly out. Browne ran the tape for Conte with the click track going at the same time. Eventually Browne realized he made a mistake. Conte was exactly "on the beat" while the rest of the band were totally off. This brought a gigantic smile of relief to Conte's face!

The evening ended with 'Love Is Strange' seguing into crowd favourite 'Stay' - both songs sharing the same turnaround chord structure - and Lindley's "high pitched" falsetto line bringing rapturous applause from the audience. The trio returned for another encore, closing the set at around 10.15pm with the introspective 'Looking East', making for the perfect closer.

As Browne sang: *"These times are famine for the soul/ while for the senses it's a feast/And there's a God-sized hunger/ Underneath the questions of the age/And an absence of light in the deepening night/Where I wait for the sun looking east"*.

I couldn't help but feel a sense the urgency in Browne's poignantly heartfelt lyrics upon the then state of world affairs…

20 - IT'S A LONG WAY THERE

Formed in 1975, Little River Band went on to become one of the first of a handful of Australian acts to achieve commercial success on a grand scale in the United States, with sales of over 30 million records in the late 70s. With rich and textured harmonies which evoked the sounds of Southern California and of such bands as The Eagles (the late Glenn Frey once called the band, 'the best singing band in the world') and Crosby, Stills and Nash, the band enjoyed a run of US Top 10 hits, with their now signature song, 'Reminiscing' garnering the band their biggest success, reaching #3 on the US charts. The song has gone on to become forever identified with the band and etched into the American psyche. It was also cited by legends such as John Lennon and Frank Sinatra as one of their favourite songs. Though the band only ever undertook one tour of the UK in 1977 and never achieved the heights of success there as they did in the US, London proved pivotal in the formation of the band, as it was there where several of the founding members first met while they had been touring with their pre-Little River Band bands.

In the wake of their huge international success, numerous personnel changes followed from the early 1980s onwards. The band's English born lead vocalist Glenn Shorrock departed in 1982 and was replaced by John Farnham – also English born - who then departed in 1986 for a solo career, hitting pay dirt with his 1986 album *Whispering Jack* which holds the record for being the biggest selling Australian album of all time in his native country. Shorrock returned in 1987 only to exit again in 1996 before legal issues surfaced leading to the original members of Little River Band losing their right to the band name in the early 2000s. This in turn led its three main principles: Beeb Birtles, Glenn Shorrock and Graeham Goble to form Birtles-Shorrock-Goble or better known under the acronym of BSG, in early 2002. It was this newly formed outfit that I was assigned to interview in June 2003.

I was dispatched to Deluxe Audio rehearsal studios in South Melbourne and having got there a little early I managed to catch the trio midway through rehearsal with their full band. As they were expecting me I quietly walked into their room just as they launched into their 1978 classic, 'Reminiscing'. It was a privilege to watch them perform this song up close and personal. I was amazed how tight and fresh they sounded, with the band comprised largely of local well-seasoned session players and those signature Little River Band harmonies were still very much evident. After they had finished the song, they worked through some vocal harmonies before downing tools to take a break for lunch. It was then that I formally introduced.

Shorrock, who was unshaven and wearing a cap and dressed in a pair of sweat pants, looked a little dishevelled while Birtles and Goble were dressed casually yet looked neat and tidy. They both looked fantastic for their age too. While I found Birtles and Goble warm and genuine and friendly, Shorrock had a little bit more of an edge to him, though he was just as friendly and genuine as the other two.

After returning from lunch Birtles, Shorrock and myself found a quiet area in the studio, where we sat down.

Though the past few years had been tumultuous for the trio with all the legal wrangling and court appearances, they were happy to discuss any topic of interest related to Little River Band. I asked Birtles whether in hindsight he had any regrets in how Shorrock was ousted from the band in 1982, the event causing inner band relations to further splinter. "When we had just finished recording *Time Exposure* (1981) we had been on the road for like eight years and recording an album every year and it was Glenn who suggested at the time that we should all take a year off, go our separate ways, and then come back together again. But we didn't listen. Looking back at it now, I realize that it was what we should have done. So it was a big mistake".

With many of Little River Band's contemporaries treading the nostalgia circuit forming Birtles-Shorrock-Goble was perfect timing. "Nostalgia has always been good business and it doesn't matter what era you pick" stated Shorrock before adding, "according to one source, 'Crosby Stills and Nash' were the biggest grossing live act last year in America".

After the interview they invited me to stay and watch the reminder of the rehearsal, but I had to politely decline as I had to be elsewhere. As I left Goble walked past me as he made his way back to the room and on the spur of the moment, I asked him about 'Reminiscing' and how he played it on guitar. "How about I show you how I play it", came his reply which was an unexpected but welcome surprise. It was like being offered a personal guitar lesson from the songwriter himself. So we returned to the rehearsal room where he kindly sat down and ran through the song for me showing me the chords and how they were played on guitar. He explained that the song's chords were actually a lot simpler to play than they sounded and for a song that at the time had just notched up 4 million air plays in America (as of 2021 it had amassed over 5 million air plays) he revealed that it had only taken him 20 minutes to write, and was inspired by his love of the old black and white movies from 1940s and 1950s and the jazz of the era, it was a memory I will forever cherish.

A month later I was invited by BSG to their dress rehearsal at The Forum, they were running through their show there on the next two evenings. Arriving around 8pm for an 8:30pm start, the place already had around 300 people in attendance, most of which were comprised of family, friends, competition winners and media as both nights were being recorded for a live DVD for a scheduled release later in the year, the place was filled with film crew who were also filming the dress rehearsal.

The show opened with a montage of their early years with Shorrock later joking, "Did you like the clips? I get to revisit my hair every night!" which brought much laughter from the audience. The hits-laden set included selected album tracks along with four new songs which the band were debuting. One new song, 'Photogenic" sounded very '80s ala 'Night Owls'. The band played for around two hours with a fifteen minute intermission in the middle. After the intermission they returned and performed an acoustic set that included 'The Other Guy' which Shorrock jokingly remarked after the song had finished, "whatever happened to that other guy?" (referring to John Farnham who had replaced Shorrock in the band in 1982). Introducing 'Seine City' Shorrock said, tongue in cheek, that it was "about an affair I once had with a Swedish model whose name was Bjorn!"

The fun continued. Hilariously Shorrock kept getting his album numbers wrong, "This is from our second album", to which Birtles intervened saying, "No, it's from the first!" The show was perfect though and after a brilliant encore that included 'Cool Change' and 'Lonesome Loser', it ended to rapturous applause. With the legal issues concerning the ownership of their name ongoing, Shorrock reiterated that "we aren't the Little River Band, but we bloody well sound like it!" The show finished around 11:15pm.

I was again invited by the band in late October of that year to see their next show at the Concert Hall, a two and half thousand seater venue that was also home to the Melbourne Symphony Orchestra and was later renamed Hamer Hall, in honour of the late former long-serving Premier of Victoria Sir Rupert Hamer.

Though that evening's show had a good attendance, it was short of a full house, and unlike the previous shows I had seen back in July, the audience this time was more subdued, and the show itself was marred by a string of technical issues. While the band were midway through 'Soul Searching' the technical issues began as a loud crackling and distorted noise rumbled through the in-house PA system. The band's manager quickly headed towards the stage to signal to the band onstage the sound issues. As soon as they ended the song, their manager requested the band take an intermission so the technical crew could have time to rectify it.

Eventually they returned to the stage and continued with the show but again, as he had done at previous shows, Shorrock, this time dressed in a flowery, purple shirt and black trousers, commented to the audience, 'we're not the Little River Band' and jokingly added a directive to any lawyers that may have been present in the audience to, 'leave us alone'. Later in the set he introduced each of the band members and when he got round to Goble he jokingly introduced him as 'Stephen Housden'. The set included a couple of different numbers compared to their July Forum shows, and the regular set staples were performed with a different feel and approach but when the technical issues returned it was decided to cut the show short although not before the band had everyone up on their seats and dancing in the aisles .

They apologized for the sound problems and thanked the audience for their support and left the stage to much loud applause. The band quickly departed the venue through the back entrance. They headed interstate to Adelaide in South Australia the next morning where they performed the show at Her Majesty's Theatre.

I next caught up with the band three years later in September 2006. This time it was on a glorious Saturday afternoon in Melbourne. The band were in town for their last show (which was sold-out) of their tour at the plush surrounds of The Palms On Crown located inside Melbourne's Crown Casino. Holding around 900 people and fully seated, it was the perfect setting for a BSG show. I'd been trying to hook up with Beeb Birtles again over the prior few weeks, to find a window in his very hectic schedule so that we could catch up over a coffee. After a number of calls we finally settled on meeting before the show on the day. The band had arrived in Melbourne the previous day and when I called Birtles in the evening to confirm a time, he happened to be at a dinner party. We agreed to meet the next day at sound check. He also told me he was flying home to the States on Sunday so time was tight.

Unfortunately upon my arrival at sound check, I was told by the band's manager that Birtles had come down with a nasty virus and due to his ill health would not be able to make it. Instead he had to rest and save his energy for the night's performance. As Goble and Shorrock prepared to sound check without Birtles, I got into a conversation with Shorrock who revealed he was busier than ever with his side projects and was planning to release an acoustic album early in the New Year. It seemed every artist of any worth was going the acoustic route at the time, a trend that was proving quite prolific for many of the artists and acts, with many big name acts from the past few decades getting their careers revived by recording and performing acoustic take-offs on their well-known classic hits. The Melbourne-based Liberation Blue record label had a series of albums that were leading the charge. Obviously acoustic albums are cheaper to make and touring in an acoustic format is a lot cheaper as well so the monetary return is bigger for all parties involved.

After chatting to Shorrock, I chatted to Goble who told me he had a new solo album out too. He shared the latest news that legal problems were still rearing their ugly head in regards to the whole Little River Band legal fight which was ongoing courtesy of former Little River Band guitarist Stephen Housden who owned the band name outright. With Birtles sick, Goble outlined the possible scenario of getting some of the band members to help provide a boost in the vocal department to help Birtles because of his illness. Suggestions were made that in the event of Birtles's condition preventing him from singing the lead on 'The Night Owls', there would be a need for one of the other guys to do it instead. The problem, as Goble explained it, was that if one member of a band such as BSG, who rely heavily on a vocal ensemble, gets sick then the main foundation of the band could get thrown into disarray. Instrumentally, if a musician is ill, a replacement is easy as any instrument can be covered or replaced but when it comes to vocals, it is an entirely different scenario.

As the sound check finally got underway, the band played through the intro of 'It's A Long Way There' so that house engineer [Ern Rose] could get everything right. Because Goble had to speed off home early in order to get changed, he quickly ran through an acoustic check with the vocals only and then once done, departed soon after. Before launching into a full blown sound check, the band played around with a version of The Beatles' 'Come Together'. It was around this time that they again invited me to stay for the full sound check but I had to decline again as I had a prior engagement. I was informed though that a lot of the band members' own allocated tickets had to be given up due to the demand in tickets for the show.

As I walked the foyer, I found Goble frantically pacing about trying to find his way back to his car. I offered to help him and he explained he was unfamiliar with the Casino and it being such a massive complex, was confused as to where he had parked his car. Eventually one of the crew came out and escorted him back to his car.

Though the trio have never announced a break-up, nothing more was heard of them after late 2007. An all American line-up of Little River Band led by Bassist/vocalist Wayne Nelson, who had joined the band in 1980 and which features none of the original members, continue to tour the States on the back of the work and legacy created by the original.

21 - ALT-ROCK STRIKES OUT

While Nirvana was the first band to initiate the genre known as Grunge into the popular mainstream, the template for it can be traced back years earlier to alt-rockers Dinosaur Jr. led by the rather subdued J. Mascis, himself the ultimate icon for the slacker generation. While having a reputation for being a man of very few words for the media, when it came to expressing himself with his band it was quite the opposite, playing a style of music that was abrasive and ear-splittingly loud. Dinosaur Jr split in the late 1990s and would reunite in 2005 and in the meantime Mascis formed a new outfit; J. Mascis + The Fog. It was while he was touring Australia in May 2003 in support of his second studio outing with his new band, 2002's *Free So Free,* that I finally got to meet him.

The art-deco Prince Of Wales hotel in St Kilda is home to a bar, a restaurant and a live music room known as Prince Bandroom where I've witnessed many bands play. As I walked in Mascis's publicist was sitting in one of the booths waiting for me. As we greeted each other, she informed me that this was going to be the first time that she'd even met Mascis and told me that he was currently in the middle of a phone interview in his hotel room.

Moments later he appeared in the bar walking towards me while talking on his phone. We are introduced to each other and he grunts 'hi' to us. With his long grey hair, lanky stature, and glasses, he looked like an eccentric older uncle. His colour co-ordinated fashion sense of matching purple shirt and runners, further emphasised his unconventional character. We decide to conduct the interview elsewhere so walk to a popular café 'Il Fornaio' next door and take our seats. The place is very noisy and buzzing with activity so I place my Dictaphone on the table to record the interview. I express some concerns that the atmosphere may be too much and will prevent much of the interview to be recorded clearly. Mascis agrees that the place is very loud so grabs my Dictaphone and proceeds to position it as close as possible to his mouth and holds it there for the entire interview. He whispers his answers making things hard to hear, so I move as close as possible to him so that he can hear my questions and I can hear his answers. His face exudes a constant 'stoned full-time' look as he stares straight at you. One and two word syllables in the form of 'ums', 'ohs' and 'not really', form much of his vocabulary.

He tells me that he was awoken at 6am by his phone and I suggested that he should have turned his phone off so he couldn't have been disturbed. Mascis responds by saying that back home no one rang him at that time and I reminded him of the time difference. After this shaky start I soon find common ground the moment I start asking him about guitars – immediately he becomes animated. The interview turns out better than expected and the guy I was talking to by the end of the interview seemed to be a completely different person to the one I'd struggled to get a sentence out of at the start! I thanked him for his time and mention that I would be seeing his show later that evening. He adds that he's been in the country for a week so far and is still struggling to get over the jet lag before heading off to the next interview.

Later that evening at his show at the Corner Hotel in Richmond I arrive around 9pm to catch the support acts before Mascis finally hits the stage at 11:30pm. The room is full to capacity and he is still wearing in the same purple outfit he had on earlier! He takes hold of his acoustic guitar, plugs it into his pedal board, takes a seat on the centre of the stage and begins to play his set. Again, he doesn't speak much during the entire 75 minute performance, allowing his music to do the talking instead. The set is peppered with a selection of material both old and new as well as a good selection of material off *Free So Free*. He plays most of the songs with a capo rather than the usual down tuned guitar.

He occasionally starts a song with just the chord progression, playing it a number of times as he records it into his Looper pedal after which he begins to play improvised solos over it. For a solo set of just acoustic guitar and vocals, it sounds remarkably good and his lead playing understates the minimalist approach of melody. His acoustic guitar is plugged into a distortion pedal which recreates his signature sound. At the start I positioned myself at the front of the stage but half way through I decide to shift to the back to take in the overall atmosphere. After his set is over, he quietly stands up and leaves the stage as the crowd scream for an encore. He returns a few moments later and performs an encore before finishing the show proper to rapturous applause.

Grunge became the soundtrack to the Nineties, yet like all new genres it soon splintered into sub-genres such as post-grunge while its influence permeated into the burgeoning nu-metal scene. Post-grunge was more refined, less abrasive and more accessible exemplified by bands such as Foo Fighters, Creed, Bush, Matchbox Twenty and Fuel. Led by main principal songwriter and guitarist Carl Bell, Fuel had been honing its craft since first coming together in the early 1990s but finally found popularity via their 1998 full-length debut album, *Sunburn* and its single 'Shimmer' which became a rock radio staple. I remember hearing the song every time I turned on the radio, and it still held strong a year later.

The band followed up with 2000's *Something Like Human* and three years later with *Natural Selection* by which time cracks began to appear in the band. It was while the band, or should I say, two of the main members, vocalist Brett Scallions and Bell were on an acoustic promo run for their recently released *Natural Selection* album in September of 2003 that I got to meet and interview them. The group had last been in Australia as part of their very first Australian tour back in 2000, when they toured in support of their *Something Like Human* album.

On the day of my interview at the Como Hotel I saw Lou Reed breeze out of the hotel foyer, but with a reputation for being shirty and having a documented distaste for idle chatter I refrained from greeting him as he jumped straight into a waiting car. Reed was in town as part of an Australian tour in support of his 2003 album *The Raven*. The swiftness of his departure, as though he was escaping a chasing mob, meant I was not able to recognise anyone with him, though it most likely would have included his long-time Tai Chi master Ren Guang-Yi who had been by his side for many years and his wife Laurie Anderson.

The star-spotting continued in the foyer when Australian Sixties pop-star Normie Rowe walked straight past me and out through the hotel entrance. He was greeted by a couple fans outside who soon started taking photos. Afterwards, as I walked out of the hotel after my interview with Fuel was done, I ran into 1970s pop diva

Marcia Hines. Though neither of us had ever met or knew each other I quickly let out a 'Hi, my name is Joe and it is nice to meet you'. Expressing surprise, she replied 'oh, hi and nice to meet you too' and walked away. I would imagine she was probably thinking 'who the hell was that!'

Anyway, back to the interview - the Sony publicist greeted me and introduced Scallions and Bell. As soon as introductions were done, Scallions was escorted to a side room where he was scheduled for a phone interview and, left alone with Bell, we engaged in some small talk as we took our seats. A small table had been set up in the room where a plate of cakes and an assortment of biscuits were laid out for the media and band to enjoy. He was very enthusiastic and gave me a good interview and was forthcoming. He also looked very much as he did in the band's videos and photos. I say this as there are many times when artists you meet look nothing like they do in their photos since most of the time it's always a polished look for mass consumption and on other occasions, images are airbrushed, but that was not the case with Bell or Scallions. At the time I had no idea of the tensions brewing inside the band, although I sensed a coolness between the pair. This would later present itself publicly when drummer Kevin Miller was dismissed from the band the following year before, not long after, Scallions also left.

As my interview with Bell came to an end, Scallions returned and took a seat in one of the opposite corners of the room to do a face to face interview with another journalist. Then the pair were informed by their publicist that they would have one more interview (which Scallions was now about to begin) before they would take a break for lunch after which they would be heading off to a radio station to do further interviews. Their visit to Melbourne was quite a quick stopover as they had been scheduled to fly out to Sydney the following day where they were to stay for a few more days before their Australian promo visit would come to an end and they could make their way back home. While in Sydney they performed a special Garage Acoustic Session, showcasing tracks from their new album for one of the major radio stations.

I next caught up with Bell four years later this time via a phone interview. The band had just released their fourth album *Angels And Devils*, which featured a new singer, Toryn Green. With Scallions now gone and Green in his place he was excited about the new line-up and new album. At one point I asked him about the general perception of Fuel, especially after Scallion's departure, that the band was basically just him. "You can't help what people think anyway and it's a waste of time to even try," he replied, "anybody that does know about our situation knows that I've written almost everything, the lyrics and the music and handle a majority of what's going down. But that doesn't mean I can do it by myself either. I like to have guys around me that can help as well and that I can help them as well". The band changes continued in 2010 when Bell himself departed and Scallions returned with a completely new line-up. And then in 2020 Scallions again left the band, which saw Bell back in charge with another new line-up.

No band defined post-grunge's mixture of angst and pop sensibilities as much as Matchbox Twenty who first came to prominence via their 1996 debut album *Yourself or Someone Like You*. Songs such as 'Push' and '3 A.M' propelled the band to international success. In late 2007 the band released *Exile On Mainstream* - a compilation of their greatest hits along with a bunch of brand new studio tracks and the band toured Australia in April 2008 in support of the album. It was on this visit that I got to meet the band and see their show. Prior to this I had interviewed the band a number of times during the 2000s over the phone and had last seen them perform live in concert in 2003, the last time they had toured Australia.

Warner Music Australia had offered me a last minute interview with Matchbox Twenty after one of the radio people who were scheduled to interview them pulled out. With interviews with the band hard to come by I wasn't going to let the opportunity pass by. Along with the interview I was also allocated tickets to the band's show at Rod Laver Arena which included a meet 'n' greet with the band backstage pre-show.

It was a warm autumn day as I arrived at the upmarket Park Hyatt Hotel which was a hive of activity with all the band interviews running slightly behind, which meant my scheduled early morning appointment was pushed back an hour. I wasn't the only one waiting around in the foyer, there were other media personnel there including such high profile media personalities as Hamish Blake from the *Hamish and Andy Show* and the entertainment editor from the *Herald-Sun*.

Finally I was invited to wait outside a large suite buzzing with activity before eventually being allowed in. As I entered I noticed one section of the room was setup purposely for interviews with guitarist Kyle Cook and Yale but both were in the midst of doing an interview with an online music site. In another area an Australian *Take 40* radio crew were packing up their gear after their interview had wrapped up and in yet another both Rob Thomas (lead vocalist) and Paul Doucette (drummer) were being interviewed by another journalist.

With their interview over both Thomas and Doucette got up and as they wandered past Cook and Yale, they began laughing out loud. Cook abruptly stopped his interview and called out, "Hey guys we're trying to do an interview here!" Thomas quickly answered Cook with some hilarious remark which from where I was standing, I could not decipher, but whatever he said sent the entire room into laughter. Once the laughter subsided, Cook resumed the interview, while Thomas ventured outside to have a cigarette. The record label people were making their presence felt everywhere to make sure things ran to schedule.

Finally it was my turn. I got introduced first to Yale who asked me whether I minded if he smoked during our interview, "No problem" I replied. So off he went to find an ashtray, in the meanwhile Cook came over and we were introduced. I began our interview by asking them about their assortment of guitars they used and this question brought much excitement to the pair. They seemed to enjoy discussing all things guitars and gear and went into great detail. I had been allotted 15 minutes but we went over time although the record label people didn't seem to mind so I ended up getting a 25 minute interview with them both. After a quick photo they moved onto their next interview. I was later informed that the band were only doing nine interviews that day and they all had to be done within an hour which was why interview slots were broken up into groups of two band members per interview.

Later that afternoon I arrived at Rod Laver Arena for the scheduled meet and great. My wife Liz and I made our may to the backstage areas stage door to wait to be escorted inside. There were only about 15 people waiting with us, comprised of invite-only radio people, retailers and some fan competition winners. We were eventually ushered into one of the large rooms where we could hear the band sound checking. We were divided into groups of four so that the band could meet, sign and get pics with everyone. It's the way we were told that the band preferred it to be done. My wife and I chatted with a couple of radio guys from Star FM who had been placed together with us to form our group. After waiting for around 25 minutes the band finally arrived having finished their sound check.

The meet and greet lasted for more than half an hour. When Yale and Cook – who was still wearing the same hat he had on earlier during our interview - approached us, Yale gave me one look and said, "Hey Joe" and raised his hand to give me a high five. Later Thomas asked me, "weren't you in the hotel room earlier?" I replied "yes" and both Cook and Yale added, "we did a guitar interview with him". I was impressed that Thomas had remembered me from just seeing me just once given the amount of interviews they must have carried out. With the mood now really relaxed, Thomas began talking to my wife and told her some jokes as Yale mentioned that he had been to a vintage guitar shop on Chapel Street in South Yarra earlier that afternoon and then suddenly in the middle of telling me this, he stopped and called out to Cook, "What was that Gretsch guitar we saw there today, was it a Tennessean?" he asked. "Yeah" came the response from Cook.

Moments later Paul Doucette, the band's former drummer, came over to join us and I asked him about how he felt having switched from being the band's drummer to now also playing guitar. "It's more of an exposed role," he admitted, "where you can't hide behind the kit, so you're out there with a guitar and it seems weird". The band really knew how to work the room, and all of them were friendly and their feel good spirits were hugely infectious to everyone present.

Time was now running away from us and with the band needing to ready themselves for the show, we were quickly ushered out of the venue through the corridor and past the night's support act Thirsty Merc's, an Australian pop-rock band who were enjoying chart success at the time. We'd been told all the Matchbox Twenty members had their wives with them on the tour as well, though we had not seen any of them backstage. We made our way through the tiered row of seating to find our allocated VIP seat located close to the stage area, and took our seats and watched the show. The evening's show was the first of two consecutive Melbourne shows while a was added two weeks later. Matchbox Twenty kicked off the night's show with their latest single 'All Your Reasons' before playing a hits laden set that included new songs off the recent *Exile On Mainstream* release.

EPILOGUE - LOUDER THAN WORDS

When I began my music journalism career at the beginning of the 21st century, the field had already evolved from its halcyon days of the 1970s and 1980s where print magazines such as *Creem*, *Circus* and *Rolling Stone* in the US and *New Musical Express*, *Melody Maker* and *Sounds* in the UK were meeting a hunger for articles about musical heroes which didn't attract attention from mainstream newspapers and radio. Yet as the internet continued to expand, especially in the early years of the 2000s, many of the print editions of these august publications began having an online presence before disappearing from news stands altogether a decade or so later.

The internet provided another outlet for music journalism. This explosion in online writing took a heavy toll on the print side of things. Bloggers became the norm, and experienced and specialized writers found themselves competing with less experienced but passionate fans of bands who wanted desperately to have an outlet away from the mainstream press to indulge their obsession. This led to a steady decline in circulation and readership for many of the print mainstays that eventually saw many close shop; some moved purely to an online presence while others sadly went out of business. Those that remained now catered for a niche market for those that still wanted their music fix in a tangible form rather than a quick, abridged blog post.

These days, as print magazines face further decline and

writing moves toward online content only, a writer faces a daily balancing act of straddling the need for clickbait headlines in order to appease an outlet's advertisers whilst at the same writing pieces that continue to satisfy the need for decent, well-researched and informed music articles but it is no different to the chnages in any other line of work over the past 20 years.

One of the huge benefits online music journalism has over traditional print - and I'm talking magazines here rather than newspapers - is its immediacy. The music business is fast-paced and print magazines usually adhere to working to a minimum three-month gap between filing your latest interview to it finally appearing in print and on store shelves and by the time it appears, it could be old news, which is why music journalists are given album advances and notice of upcoming releases and interview opportunities months in advance in order to work to this integral time line deadline. The purpose of it is to tie in the eventual publication of the interview, music article, review or other piece of writing, to as close as possible to the release date of the artist's album or whatever new project the artist has coming out. This way it remains relevant and up to date and they reap maximum promotional benefit from it. In today's age of instant gratification, and in the way music is also quickly consumed, you can literally undertake an interview, write it up, send it to your editor and it can be online within hours – far faster than a print newspaper.

I have always first and foremost been a musician, and with music journalism in general being affected on all fronts from the changes that the industry was going through, I shifted my focus to concentrating on my playing career predominantly. From the late 1980s I had been playing guitar for numerous cover bands with stints in a couple of original outfits. During the whole period I was undertaking a journalism career, I was also playing guitar in my own covers band, DoubleVision. Eventually I got tired of playing covers and a desire to write my own music was reignited. In the years prior I had written songs and recorded several demos of vocal material and I returned to them to see what I could do with them as well as beginning to write fresh material with the goal of eventually recording and releasing them commercially.

In late 2010 I released my debut solo single, an acoustic instrumental outing titled 'Travellin' West'. As I enjoyed noodling around on the guitar, I came up with this piece one day after many hours of playing around. It is a multi-layered piece within a very melodic frame work that echoed the spirit of travelling on the wide open roads of America.

My magazine connections helped me initially achieve some good press for the release, although being on the other side of the pen reminded me of the hardships an artist endures, especially for an independent artist like myself, in order to build and sustain a full-time playing career and a relationship with the media. Just because I was a music journalist it didn't make my path any easier, in fact I found any kind of support from my previous magazine connections largely lacking, especially when it came to Australia but I was determined to make it purely on my own musical terms, and not because I already had a name in media.

In May 2011 I released an all-instrumental electric guitar track, 'Face Off', as a single. Little did I know that the release of this track would start a chain of events that led me to being signed to a European label and onto my first ever European tour, the first of many I would embark on during the next decade. Somehow the single caught the ears of Alex Wieser of Austrian-based record label W.A.R. Productions. A one-man operation, his label had released numerous folk-ambient and underground metal outings over the years. He expressed an interest in my music, really liked what he heard and offered me a deal.

So I wrote and recorded an all-instrumental rock EP titled *Slave To The Fingers* as my first offering to the label and by way of introducing myself to guitar-loving audiences. The label put the EP out on CD in November 2011. The interest garnered by the release and with plans to release further music through the label, led to discussions of going over to Europe for a small tour that would take in dates in Austria and the UK.

Over the next six months we discussed and organised the tour, which we locked in for September-October 2012. In the meantime I went back into the studio to write and record my first full length album, *Creature Of Habit,* another largely instrumental album, but which also featured my first ever vocal outing on the track 'Fallen Angel', a song I originally wrote and demoed back in 2001 and which would become my signature song in Europe.

I flew out of Melbourne's Tullamarine Airport on the afternoon of September 18 2012 to embark on my first ever European tour. The long haul flight took around 30 hours, finally arriving the next day in Vienna. The flight took me to Singapore and then onto Heathrow airport where I then caught a connecting flight to Austria's capital. With picture perfect weather, and with a window seat, I took in the breathtaking view of the landscape below on my flight path as the plane made its way over the UK,

France, Belgium, Germany and finally into Austrian air space. Upon arrival at Vienna I was met by Alex who was there to pick me up and escort me to his home. After grabbing a bite, Alex drove me around for a brief tour of some of the amazing sights of Vienna, before we made our way back to his home in Linz which was about a two hour drive west of Vienna. Alex would be alongside me for the entire three-week duration of that first European tour.

With only a few days to go before my first ever European show on the Saturday, I relaxed and tried to get over the jet lag which had supremely kicked in. I spent time with Alex and his family and acquainted myself with Austrian culture and cuisine. On the day before my first show, we ventured out to Ruine Schaunburg, a 12th century castle nestled above the mountains outside of Linz, to spend the afternoon shooting footage for the film clip to 'Fallen Angel' which would be released as a single later that year. The day was picture perfect, with nothing but clear blue skies and no tourists at the site.

Show day finally arrived, with most of the day from late morning onward spent at the venue preparing for the evening's performance, meeting the other musicians and artists who were sharing the festival bill where I was the headline act and sound checking. As show time approached, I hit the stage to a full house, it was a remarkable feeling, being my first ever appearance outside of Australia, and quite an emotional and joyous occasion. The night's show was an acoustic set of my original material thus far that began with the instrumental 'Travellin' West' and closed with 'Fallen Angel'. Each song was well received with much applause and after 'Fallen Angel', the audience erupted into a choir of calls of 'Mehr' (German for 'more') for an encore. The audience were absolutely wonderful to perform to and very responsive and I was deeply moved to have been accepted with open arms. It had been a great way to kick off my inaugural European tour in style.

The next day we boarded a flight to London where the next leg of the tour would kick off. I would be performing two shows in the UK; one in Lancaster and the other in Bolton. We were met at Stansted airport upon arrival by my UK tour manager David John who also kindly doubled as my chauffeur. We crashed for the night at his home in Guildford before a four hour drive to Lancaster in the north of England where we'd be for the week. In the days leading up to my next show my schedule was busy with early morning radio interviews and press engagements, and a solid full day's rehearsal at one of Lancaster's rehearsal studios with a local band I had tapped to be my backing band for the shows.

The morning of the show was spent exploring the delights of Morecambe Bay before heading out in the late afternoon to The Bobbin in Lancaster to sound check and prepare for the night's performance. The Bobbin's live music stage was inside the pub's front area that featured a decent size stage and welcoming atmosphere that was underscored by an air of intimacy. I was chuffed to find two dedicated female fans from Sweden had flown all the way over to the UK to catch both of my shows!

After the support band had finished I finally hit the stage around 10.30pm, playing a 70 minute all electric set that featured material from both my EP and *Creature Of Habit* album along with a couple covers. Exhausted and pleased with the show we headed back to base. The next day we all hit the highway again and headed for Manchester, for a well-deserved day off to take in the sights of the city and its cuisine and to catch up with long time friend - writer and acclaimed author Mick Middles.

Show day #2 finally came around and this time the venue was a cavern style setting called The Alma Inn in downtown Bolton. A lively and friendly place, it was abuzz with a hardcore metal and rock music clientele that slowly swelled in numbers as the evening wore on. We finally hit the stage around 11pm and played a blinding and very loud set to rapturous applause.

The next day we hit the road again for the long drive back to London. We eventually clocked up 1,500 km in the car in the UK alone. Back in London we added two last minute impromptu acoustic performances in Camden to my itinerary following press interest. An early evening set at Camden Eye, after which Alex and I rushed out in the pouring rain to the next show later that same evening at The Abbey Tavern about a kilometre away, both of us unaware that a bus was available! The audience at both venues were appreciative and responsive.

The next day was spent having a nice relaxing lunch with my good friend Steve Harley. Afterwards it was off to Soho for a couple of interviews with London-based music magazines. It had been an exhausting week with four UK shows and press duties, so for the remaining few days we decided to make our way over to Hamburg to connect with some industry people to discuss plans for making inroads with my music into the German market.

The last day of our German stay saw us up early before daybreak to catch our flights home. I boarded a flight to London and then spent the next few hours waiting at Heathrow before boarding my flight back to Australia. Upon arrival in the early hours of the next morning at Sydney airport, daylight savings had come into effect in Australia the day prior and because I was unaware of that, I missed my flight back to Melbourne but luckily I managed to catch the next one.

After 48 hours without much sleep and going through five countries I finally arrived home totally exhausted. Touring is a strenuous undertaking, very time consuming and takes every bit of energy you have. For the most part, that hour and half on stage is all the audience see. The other remaining twenty-two or so hours are spent travelling, doing press, eating and sleeping. It's certainly not a glamorous lifestyle and one I already knew from my many years of interviewing artists and being behind the scenes with them. On my next tour, in 2014, I performed twelve shows that were fitted into a tight three-week schedule spread across six countries. It was one of the most arduous tours I have ever embarked upon. I came home five kilos lighter!

The world pandemic of 2020 completely changed things around again in music journalism, and for the music industry in general. While interviews previously had been conducted mostly face to face, now it shifted to an online format and remotely where Zoom interviews suddenly became the new norm and with touring off the cards due to country borders being shut, musicians began utilizing the internet with live streaming events, remote recording and anything else they could come up with in order to stay active.

As with everything in life, music journalism will continue to evolve and move into uncharted waters we are yet to know. Who knows where it will be in ten years time but one thing is certain, music will always be around and there will always be a thirst from the fans of having a shared experience of wanting to know more about their favourite artists and the music they create.

Joe Matera